FINANCING SMALL AND MEDIUM-SIZED ENTERPRISES IN ASIA AND THE PACIFIC

CREDIT GUARANTEE SCHEMES

MARCH 2022

ASIAN DEVELOPMENT BANK

© 2022 Asian Development Bank
6 ADB Avenue, Mandaluyong City, 1550 Metro Manila, Philippines
Tel +63 2 8632 4444; Fax +63 2 8636 2444
www.adb.org

Some rights reserved. Published in 2022.

ISBN 978-92-9269-358-9 (print); 978-92-9269-359-6 (electronic); 978-92-9269-360-2 (ebook)
Publication Stock No. TCS220030-2
DOI: http://dx.doi.org/10.22617/TCS220030-2

The views expressed in this publication are those of the authors and do not necessarily reflect the views and policies of the Asian Development Bank (ADB) or its Board of Governors or the governments they represent. The findings in this publication are binding on either ADB or the governments that they represent, including the Government of India.

ADB does not guarantee the accuracy of the data included in this publication and accepts no responsibility for any consequence of their use. The mention of specific companies or products of manufacturers does not imply that they are endorsed or recommended by ADB in preference to others of a similar nature that are not mentioned.

By making any designation of or reference to a particular territory or geographic area, or by using the term "country" in this document, ADB does not intend to make any judgments as to the legal or other status of any territory or area.

Please contact pubsmarketing@adb.org if you have questions or comments with respect to content, or if you wish to obtain copyright permission for your intended use that does not fall within these terms, or for permission to use the ADB logo.

Corrigenda to ADB publications may be found at http://www.adb.org/publications/corrigenda.

Notes:
In this publication, "$" refers to United States dollars (unless otherwise stated), "B" refers to baht, "CHF" refers to Swiss francs, "€" refers to euros, "HK$" refers to Hong Kong dollars, "₹" refers to Indian rupees, "₱" refers to pesos, "£" refers to pounds sterling, "RM" refers to ringgit, "Rp" refers to rupiah, "T" refers to tenge, and "W" refers to won. ADB recognizes "China" as the People's Republic of China; "Hong Kong" as Hong Kong, China; "Korea" as the Republic of Korea; and "Hanoi" as Ha Noi.

Cover design by Cleone Baradas.

CONTENTS

TABLES, FIGURES, AND BOXES

BOXES

ACKNOWLEDGMENTS

Financing Small and Medium-Sized Enterprises in Asia and the Pacific: Credit Guarantee Schemes is a product of the Sustainable Development and Climate Change Department (SDCC) of the Asian Development Bank (ADB).

Junkyu Lee, chief of Finance Sector Group, headed a core team of staff in preparing this publication. Staff and consultants in SDCC, co-led by Sung Su Kim, financial sector specialist (Inclusive Finance) and Mohammad Shadan Khan, SME financing specialist consultant and Hyungchan Lee, financial sector specialist, SDCC, provided crucial support and coordinated production of the publication.

Operational support was graciously provided by Katherine Mitzi Co, associate operations analyst, SDCC and Matilde Mila Cauinian, operations assistant, SDCC. Additional research support was provided by Alyssa Villanueva and Mikko Marl Diaz.

The team wishes to thank representatives from the Korea Credit Guarantee Fund and the Credit Guarantee Corporation Malaysia Berhad, who participated and shared their views in the Webinar held on 29 June 2020 and made valuable suggestions for developing the publication.

The team greatly appreciates Syed Ali-Mumtaz Shah from ADB's Central and West Asia Public Management, Financial Sector, and Trade Division and Takuya Hoshino from ADB's South Asia Public Management, Financial Sector, and Trade Division for valuable comments and inputs to this publication and staff in ADB headquarters and in resident missions who contributed to the knowledge events on 29 June 2020 and 6 November 2020.

We thank all contributors for their valiant support of this publication despite the difficult situation caused by the coronavirus disease.

Finally, the team also acknowledges colleagues from the Department of Communications for their continuous support in disseminating the publication.

ABBREVIATIONS

ADB	Asian Development Bank
CGC	credit guarantee corporation
CGS	credit guarantee scheme
COVID-19	coronavirus disease
CRD	credit risk database
EU	European Union
EXIM	Export-Import Bank of Thailand
GDP	gross domestic product
KODIT	Korea Credit Guarantee Fund
KOTEC	Korea Technology Credit Guarantee Fund
MFI	microfinance institution
MSMEs	micro, small, and medium-sized enterprises
NPL	nonperforming loan
OECD	Organisation for Economic Co-operation and Development
PRC	People's Republic of China
SDCC	Sustainable Development and Climate Change Department
SMEs	small and medium-sized enterprises
UK	United Kingdom
US	United States

EXECUTIVE SUMMARY

Small and medium-sized enterprises (SMEs) are widely regarded as the backbone of economies around the world. Their contribution to gross domestic product and exports is unique and they employ a greater share of populations than many bigger enterprises, globally and in Asia. In this region, they typically comprise more than 90% of enterprises and contribute immensely to job creation and exports.

Yet, SMEs face multiple challenges in gaining access to finance that can fuel their growth, for many reasons. Several issues stand out and are discussed in this publication. Broadly speaking these include (i) that lenders perceive SMEs as risky borrowers engaged in less-than-desirable organizational practices, and (ii) that such firms face regulatory bottlenecks and financial system structures in the developing countries in Asia and the Pacific that hinder their access to finance.

The publication explores these challenges and the role that credit guarantee schemes (CGSs) can play in mitigating them, especially during crises.

In the first area, SMEs typically do not follow the best financial management and corporate governance practices, which contributes to a credit assessment information asymmetry between lenders and borrowers, feeding a perception of these smaller firms as risky. As such, lenders would prefer some sort of insurance against default (i.e., collateral), but usually prefer immovable collateral that many SMEs do not possess. This is an important difficulty in these firms accessing finance.

Regulatory bottlenecks also severely hamper SME access to credit. The Basel Framework's emphasis on external ratings often results in SMEs getting a risk weight of 100% or higher, which means that the regulatory capital cost for banks, compared to AA– or better borrowers, is five times higher, undermining lending to SMEs.

SMEs also suffer in terms of provisioning, as they usually do not possess immovable collateral, which receives preferential regulatory treatment in many developing countries in Asia and the Pacific.

These regulatory hurdles were exacerbated by the introduction of liquidity and leverage frameworks after the global financial crisis of 2008–2009. These frameworks demand high-quality and liquid assets as "perceived" by the market. Due to lower credit ratings resulting from stringent regulatory policies, SMEs often have to pay a regulatory surcharge on their borrowings.

Multiple behaviors and organizational phenomena hamper the extension of credit to SMEs, including loss/regret aversion, defensive decision-making, and "satisficing"—combining the words "satisfy" and "suffice."

The end result is that without supporting public goods for credit assessment and gaps in insolvency mechanisms in the developing countries in Asia and the Pacific, banks are very wary of extending credit to SMEs.

Yet, in the developing countries in Asia and the Pacific, banks dominate the financial ecosystem, with other avenues of lending (nonbanking, capital markets, leasing and factoring, etc.) comparatively underdeveloped. According to the Asian Development Bank's (ADB) SME Monitor 2020 (ADB 2020a), MSME bank loans averaged 14.8% of gross domestic product and 16.9% of the region's total bank lending during 2010–2019, contracting at a compound annual rate of 1.3% and 0.3%, respectively. The MSME loan market is small, and its sluggish growth reflects the declining growth of national economies.

The limited development and roles of nonbanking financial institutions, capital markets, and leasing and factoring mechanisms constrain the ability of SMEs to circumvent the challenges of the relatively inflexible and daunting expectations of the banking system. Many countries (Japan, the Republic of Korea, Malaysia, and Thailand) have functioning SME capital markets and venture capital is picking up in countries such as Japan and the Republic of Korea. Overall, however, the development of nonbanking avenues of finance falls short of potential, creating challenges for SMEs.

Nonetheless, it might be possible to mitigate these issues using credit infrastructure services such as credit registries, movable collateral registries, robust insolvency mechanisms, and CGSs. While CGSs are found in most developing countries in Asia and the Pacific, scope exists for improvement in the other credit infrastructure services that could significantly boost SME access to finance.

Supporting SMEs has been a primary focus of ADB engagements with the developing countries in Asia and the Pacific, and the CGS has been a critical component of many of those engagements. The CGS is a preferable policy tool, due to its strong leverage effect achieved through guaranteed loans; its regulatory relief, available in many countries, as per the Basel framework; and the schemes' critical role during crises.

The CGS has existed in developed countries since the beginning of the 20th century, and by 2015 were present all around the globe. The CGS is widely regarded as one of the most market-friendly interventions and has proven able to improve SME access to finance in many countries, including developing countries in Asia and the Pacific.

In principle, the CGS improves SME access to finance by sharing the default risk with lenders, which mitigates information asymmetry and other management issues. To further support SMEs, many schemes also offer business and financial advisory services to help firms optimally manage their business and financial affairs, as per market expectations.

This publication examines the role of the CGS in two primary ways. First, it looks at evidence from countries across the globe to determine the impact of the CGS and, second, it scrutinizes that evidence in case studies of six countries in Asia: the People's Republic of China (PRC), India, Japan, the Republic of Korea, Malaysia, and Sri Lanka. It also examines evidence in the European Union (EU) and the United States to understand the different business models, governance practices, services offered, risk management, etc., in those regions.

The true impact of the CGS is measured by the issue of "additionality," that is, the positive impact CGS interventions have made compared to scenarios without CGS intervention. Additionality is measured on two counts: financial additionality and economic additionality. The former is more of a direct impact and assesses how much easier or favorable securing credit becomes for SMEs. The commonly used assessment metrics for financial additionality are loan approvals, loan tenor, rate of interest, reduction in collateral demanded, etc.

Economic additionality gauges the wider impact of CGS intervention by assessing the increase in investments, employment, exports, tax paid, and so on, in supported SMEs.

On both counts, financial and economic additionality and credible data from accomplished researchers around the world establish the positive impact of the CGS on SMEs.

This publication's case studies look at CGSs in detail to glean insights into the legal and regulatory setup, corporate governance, services offered, and the risk management practices adopted in diverse countries and regions. In brief, these insights include:

(i)   Differences in the organizational model were stark and reflected the political and financial system of the country. While many countries had public guarantee schemes, countries such as the Republic of Korea and Malaysia had a public–private partnership CGS model. By contrast, in the PRC and the EU, multiple credit guarantee players dominate, including private mutual guarantee schemes, which operate within the broad regulatory framework of the CGS.

(ii) The choice of risk assessment (retail versus wholesale) and organizational model affected staff strength and the professionalism of the CGS. In Asia, staff strength and management were strong in Japan, the Republic of Korea, and Malaysia.

(iii) Well-managed CGSs also offered advisory services for SMEs, which aided their functioning in the long run and made access to finance easier.

(iv) Running a CGS in a financially sustainable fashion is a challenge and it was observed that the better-managed CGSs committed to a leverage ratio and transparency about their risk and operations. Again, Japan, the Republic of Korea, and Malaysia had good risk assessment capabilities and sustainable guaranteed income, instead of depending upon budgetary allocations.

(v)   The EU, meanwhile, was noteworthy for the significant presence of private mutual guarantee schemes, formed by member SMEs allowing them to reduce information asymmetry with lending institutions in a decentralized fashion and without the active support of governments.

The case studies elucidate that, regardless of the governance model used, running a CGS professionally with adequate financial strength and prudent risk management practices is crucial to gaining market confidence in its ability to deliver financial access to SMEs.

The unique and central position of the CGS in the financial system has been widely useful in addressing the vulnerable situation of SMEs during the Asian and global financial crises and the current coronavirus disease (COVID-19) crisis, among others. This use has prevented the rapid mortality of vulnerable SMEs by providing them with new financing, relaxed repayment terms, and moratoriums through the lenders. Despite minor instances of misuse of the guarantee support extended, these mishaps can be easily prevented, as this publication discusses.

The CGS offers various tools to address cash flow issues particular to each country to help smooth cash flow over a longer horizon. CGSs have helped troubled SMEs weather crises by addressing systemic loss aversion tendencies in financial institutions and deploying policy tools such as increased guarantee coverage ratios.

To support Asia and Pacific economies, ADB has developed operational policy recommendations for the key priority areas of the CGS, focusing on legal and regulatory setup, corporate governance, services offered, risk management, and monitoring.

For the current COVID-19 crisis, these recommendations set out in structured fashion the policy tools that can be used through the CGS to limit the pandemic's adverse and lingering impacts on SME financial access. These policy recommendations provide an excellent opportunity for enhanced country partnerships to address and mitigate the impact of COVID-19 in developing countries in Asia and the Pacific.

I | INTRODUCTION

Historically, around the world, small and medium-sized enterprises (SMEs) have shown themselves to be the backbone of economies, especially in emerging markets. They drive economic growth, employment, and export revenues and, given their wider impact, their growth has been a focus area for developing countries in Asia and the Pacific.

However, SMEs have been facing insurmountable challenges in accessing finance for decades. Yet, interventions to resolve that problem, including SME credit guarantee schemes (CGSs), SME credit insurance schemes, targeted lending, interest subsidies, etc., have achieved varying success in different economies. These have led policy makers and economists to wonder if interventions are required, to what extent, and how the free market could ideally coexist with such interventions. Before examining the issue in detail, below is a brief study of the importance of SMEs, financing landscapes, and the functioning of the market.

Why SMEs Are Important—Impact on Gross Domestic Product, Employment, and Exports

A survey of 20 prominent Asian countries from 5 Asian regions shows that SMEs account for 96% of all enterprises and provide employment to 62% of workforces across these 20 countries (Yoshino and Taghizadeh-Hesary 2018a). By contribution to growth, SMEs in these 20 countries accounted for an average of 42% of gross domestic product (GDP) or manufacturing value-added (ADB 2015). By trade, the latest data indicates that SMEs contribute around 80% of the People's Republic of China's (PRC) exports; around 40% in India, the Republic of Korea, and the Kyrgyz Republic; 29% in Thailand; and 17% in Malaysia (Table 1).

Despite this critical role, SMEs still do not have a harmonized definition in Asia and the Pacific. The definition of SMEs commonly includes classification by employment, assets or capital, and revenue (sales or turnover). Indeed, the two criteria—employment and assets or capital and revenue—has been set by several economies. For example, Thailand classifies manufacturing SMEs as firms with fewer than 200 employees and less than B200 million (about $6.7 million) in fixed capital.

Countries also adopt extensive sectoral demarcation while classifying firms as SMEs. The PRC has 15 sector definitions, Japan has 4, and the Philippines has none.

Further issues arise for SMEs as national government agencies may have varying definitions. A ministry may use a particular definition, while the national statistics office works with a different one, and a priority lending policy may take on an alternative (Yoshino and Taghizadeh-Hesary 2018a).

Table 1: Snapshot of Small and Medium-Sized Enterprises' Contribution
to Selected Asian and Pacific Economies

Income Classification	Country	Enterprises (%)	Employment (%)	Exports (%)	GDP (%)
High-Income Country	Japan	99.7	70.0	NA	53.0
	Republic of Korea	99.9	89.7	37.5	51.2
Upper Middle-Income Country	People's Republic of China	NA	90.0	80.0	70.0
	Fiji	97.0	60.0	NA	18.0
	Indonesia	100	97.0	14.4	61.1
	Kazakhstan	96.3	NA	NA	28.3
	Malaysia	98.5	66.2	17.3	38.3
	Thailand	99.8	85.5	28.7	43.0
Lower Middle-Income Country	Bangladesh	99.9	85.9	NA	NA
	Cambodia	99.8	70.0	NA	58.0
	India	95.0	40.0	40.0	28.8
	Kyrgyz Republic	NA	20.5	39.3	41.5
	Lao People's Democratic Republic	97.0	63.0	NA	NA
	Mongolia	75.0	43.0	2.3	17.0
	Papua New Guinea	98.0	NA	0.7	6.0
	Philippines	99.5	63.2	25.0	35.7
	Sri Lanka	99.8	75.1	NA	52.0
	Viet Nam	97.0	77.0	NA	41.0

GDP = gross domestic product, NA = not available.

Notes: Bangladesh, Fiji, the Philippines, and Viet Nam include micro-sized enterprises. Based on latest available data: the Lao People's Democratic Republic (2013); Cambodia (2014); Malaysia (2015); Japan, the Republic of Korea, and Viet Nam (2017); the People's Republic of China, Fiji, India, Indonesia, Kazakhstan, the Kyrgyz Republic, Mongolia, Papua New Guinea, the Philippines, Sri Lanka, and Thailand (2018).

Source: Authors' compilation, based on data from government websites and multilateral research.

The Appendix gives a detailed classification criterion matrix adopted by the developing countries in Asia and the Pacific. Table 2 presents a brief classification matrix of SMEs in selected Asia and Pacific countries and Tables 3 and 4 provide the definition adopted by the World Bank Group and the European Union (EU), a widely recognized global definition.

SMEs have a very diverse profile in Asia's developing economies. There are four indicators that are widely used to determine the significance of SMEs. They identify the SME share of the total for (i) the number of enterprises, (ii) employment, (iii) domestic output, and (iv) exports. However, there are countries that compile data only on the first two indicators.

Table 2: Small and Medium-Sized Enterprise Definition in Selected Asia and Pacific Countries

| Region | Country | SME Definition | | | | | |
		Employee	Asset	Turnover	Others	By Sector	Legal Basis
Central Asia	Kazakhstan	✓	✓				✓
East Asia	People's Republic of China	✓		✓		✓	✓
	Republic of Korea	✓		✓	✓ Capital	✓	
South Asia	Bangladesh	✓	✓			✓	
	India			✓	✓ Capital	✓	✓
	Sri Lanka		✓	✓			
Southeast Asia	Cambodia	✓	✓				
	Indonesia		✓	✓			✓
	Malaysia	✓		✓		✓	✓
	Philippines	✓	✓				✓
	Thailand	✓	✓			✓	✓
	Viet Nam	✓			✓ Capital	✓	✓
Pacific	Papua New Guinea	✓					
	Solomon Islands	✓		✓			

SMEs = small and medium-sized enterprises.

Source: Asian Development Bank. 2015. *Asia SME Finance Monitor 2014*. Manila.

Table 3: World Bank Group Definition of Micro, Small, and Medium-Sized Enterprises

Indicator	Employees	Total Assets	Annual Sales	Loan Size
Micro enterprise	<10	<$100,000	<$100,000	<$10,000
Small enterprise	10–49	$100,000–$3 million	$100,000–$3 million	<$100,000
Medium-sized enterprise	50–300	$3 million–$15 million	$3 million–$15 million	<$1 million or $2 million

Source: International Finance Corporation. 2010. The SME Banking Knowledge Guide. https://www.ifc.org/wps/wcm/connect/ c6298e7b-9a16-4925-b6c0-81ea8d2ada28/SMEE.pdf?MOD=AJPERES&CVID=jkCVrZU.

Table 4: European Union Definition of Micro, Small, and Medium-Sized Enterprises

Company Category	Staff Headcount	Turnover	Balance Sheet Total
Micro enterprise	<10	≤€2 million	≤€2 million
Small enterprise	<50	≤€10 million	≤€10 million
Medium enterprise	<250	≤€50 million	≤€43 million

Source: European Union. SME Definition. https://ec.europa.eu/growth/smes/sme-definition_en.

While it is evident that SMEs play a critical role in the developing countries in Asia and the Pacific, the tabular comparison may not provide important insights into the factors in the different countries. Figure 1 is a box-plot analysis of selected Asia and Pacific countries by income. From it, it is reasonable to infer that while SMEs' share of enterprise remains the same regardless of the income classification, there is clear demarcation when it comes to contribution to employment, exports, or GDP. The income classification, ergo the presence of various institutional enablers, seems to play an important role here. The factors affecting financing will be analyzed later. In Southeast Asia, micro, small, and medium-sized enterprises (MSMEs) were reported to comprise an average of 97% of officially registered enterprises. This implies that the retention rate of SMEs is low, and it is crucial to enhance SME competitiveness to increase their contribution to domestic economies.[1]

Figure 1: **Small and Medium-Sized Enterprise Contribution to Selected Asia and Pacific Economies by Income** (%)

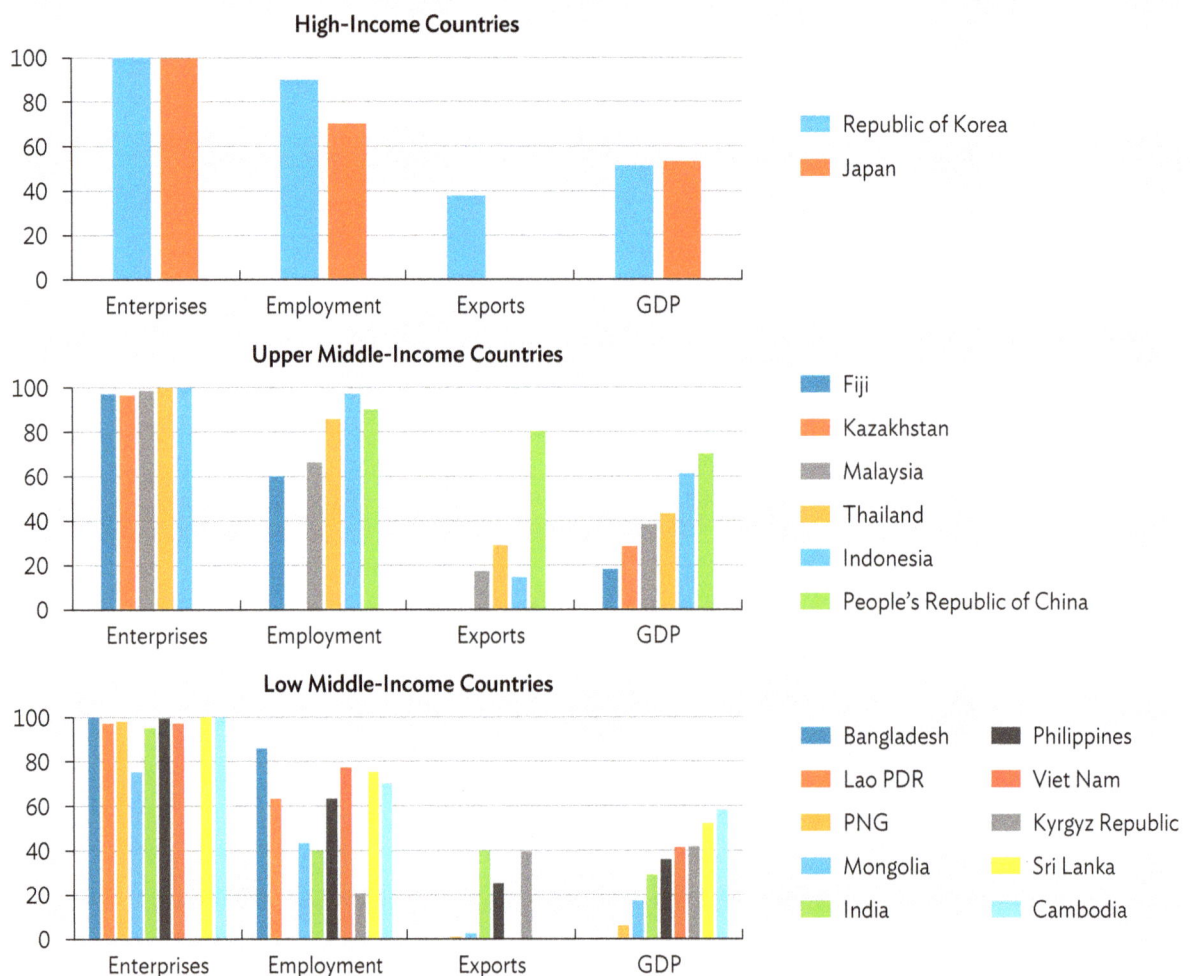

GDP = gross domestic product, Lao PDR = Lao People's Democratic Republic, PNG = Papua New Guinea, SMEs = small and medium-sized enterprises.

Source: Authors' compilation, based on data from government websites and multilateral research.

---

[1]   SME retention rate or survival rate refers to the percentage of SMEs established in a given year that remained operational after a certain period of time.

II CONTOURS OF SMALL AND MEDIUM-SIZED ENTERPRISE FINANCING

An SME needs credit to grow, and its traditional sources come from internal funds, friends, family, trade credit, and external financial institutions. The need for external credit arises basically out of cashflow mismatch issues. For businesses, cash flow for services rendered usually arises in a certain period after delivery of services. Firms need to avail of credit to capitalize on business opportunities and grow. A brief decomposition of credit assessment is elucidated in Box 1.

Box 1: **How Does Credit Assessment Happen?**

Financial institutions, while extending credit, endeavor to assess two things: (i) timely repayments over the tenure of a loan, and (ii) recouping the amount in case repayments fail (also technically known as loss given default). The broad lending practices equivalent to this would be "cash-flow-based" and "collateral-based" lending. Policy makers and regulators have been advocating for a major focus on cash-flow based lending for many years, but due to inherent limitations in external supporting credit infrastructure and human-based lending mechanisms, lending practices have been predominantly collateral-based.

A financial institution is an intermediary that connects those who save funds with those who need credit. Cost of funds is basically the sum of compensation made to the saver of funds plus a fraction of cost of operations (financial + operational). Cost of funds is determined by the business model of the bank. It is determined primarily by the funding mix of the bank and the efficiency of its asset-liability management. Profit margin is mostly determined by the market factors and, hence, predatory pricing practices are more of an issue in the financial ecosystem.

Determining risk premium is the most challenging aspect of this assessment. Broadly, this risk assessment has two cost components: the business cost associated with extending credit to a certain category of risky borrowers, and the regulatory cost (capital and provisioning) that financial institutions will incur against it. Small and medium-sized enterprises face challenges on both counts.

Cost of Credit Breakup

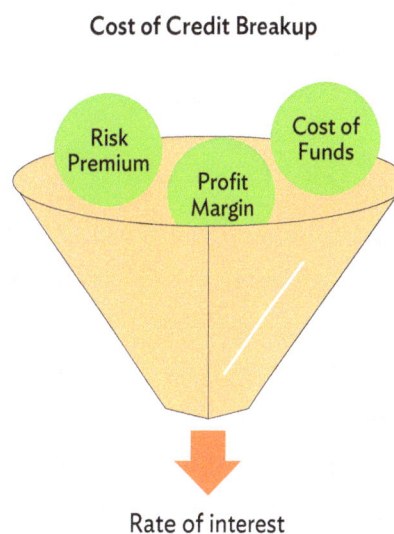

Rate of interest

Note: The cost of credit primarily comprises three components: cost of funds + risk premium + profit margin = rate of interest.

Source: Authors' summary.

Why Are SMEs Perceived as Risky Borrowers?

To reliably assess borrower risk, banks need information. The information could be static, such as turnover, firm sector, employee strengths, etc., or it could be dynamic or transactional information, such as repayment history. It is amply established that transactional characteristics are much more reliable indicators of credit behavior than the static characteristics of a firm (Owens and Wilhelm 2017). Large firms, which usually exist for longer periods, have longer transactional relationships with multiple firms, allowing financial institutions to have better risk assessment.

On the other hand, as SMEs typically do not have a relationship with financial firms and the majority of them tend to fail (bankruptcy, foreclosure, insolvency, interruption) within 5 years (OECD 2000), gaps exist in financial institutions credit assessment models for assessing SME risk premiums.

Another key challenge in credit assessment is the quality and timeliness of the financial information SMEs have. Most SMEs find it challenging to adhere to best practice; accounting standards and balance sheets are often prepared with a substantial lag of 9–12 months, weakening the reliability of credit information conveyed by these numbers.

Two additional considerations of lenders exacerbate the unfavorable credit perception of SMEs: (i) monitoring costs, and (ii) availability of collateral (World Bank 2019a). SMEs suffer unduly on these counts as financial institutions find it much easier to monitor a large enterprise with large loan exposure, with collateral provided, than SMEs that lack collateral and have much smaller loan exposure. For the same loan amount, lenders have to monitor a much higher number of SMEs, which increases their monitoring costs. Further, as noted, due to the nature of the SME industry, not many SMEs can afford to offer collateral. SMEs typically could offer movable collateral (such as vehicles, equipment, inventory, etc.) but in most countries the supporting ecosystem (credit registries, enforcement mechanism) of movable collateral is not well-developed. Movable assets such as equipment, inventories, and receivables account for around 78% of an enterprise's capital stock in the developing world, while immovable assets account for only 22%. However, as noted, financial institutions strongly prefer immovable assets as collateral for the following reasons:

- **Ease of documentation:** In almost all countries, the ecosystem related to documentation and verification of immovable assets is available, whereas the same is not available for movable assets, unless developed.

- **Ease of recovery:** It is much easier for banks to take control of immovable assets and gather a good recovery rate in the event of default. The legal and enforcement mechanisms also help in the recovery.

- **Preferential regulatory treatment:** The immovable collateral often gets preferential treatment in regulatory frameworks, which decreases the cost of lending for banks, which is also reflected in the regulatory frameworks prescribing capital requirements for regulated financial institutions. Many of a borrower's movable assets can be used as collateral by lenders operating under efficient legal settings for secured transactions. For example, an enterprise's capital stock in the United States (US) is composed of 60% movable assets while about 70% of SME-business lending in the country is related to or uses movable assets as collateral (World Bank 2019a).

Regulatory Bottlenecks in Lending to SMEs

Two key impacts that financial institutions bear when they extend a loan are keeping capital and provisions. Capital is to provide for unexpected losses associated with loans, and provisions are to be made for expected losses. The most used and desired form of capital, as per Bank for International Settlements regulations, is common equity. However, as equity is the costliest form of capital, financial institutions may not be very keen to load up on exposures, which increases the demand for common equity as capital.

Basel II regulations (BIS 2006) require banks to "risk-weight" their loan assets and then keep the capital against those risk-weighted assets. The risk weight of an asset is determined by its external credit rating (unrated/BBB+ is 100%) or internal rating model determined risk weight (for banks who have sophisticated risk management and are judged suitable by regulators to deploy the internal ratings-based approaches). In developing countries, banks generally do not have robust internal ratings-based models, due to data scarcity issues associated with SME exposures (Gottschalk 2007). Under external rating approaches, an external credit rating is granted by accredited credit rating agencies, and SMEs invariably end up getting a 100% (or worse) risk-weight associated with their exposure. Commonly, this outcome is because credit rating models used by credit rating agencies treat the universe of large companies and SMEs alike (probably as Basel regulations to date do not have a special classification for SME exposures). And SMEs, with their limited financial depth, cyclical business models, and individual-oriented corporate governance, end up getting a BBB or worse credit rating (Moody's Analytics 2016) regardless of years of cash flow and business performance. This increases the cost of funds by roughly five times for financial institutions, as risk weight is 20% until an AA– rated borrower, whereas it is 100% or worse for the unrated/BBB+ rating SMEs usually end up getting. The only limited relief under the Basel II framework is, if the SME exposure is less than €1 million, they are classified as "regulatory retail" and attract a 75% risk weight.

In examining regulation related to the cost of provisioning, similar differences are observed. Provisioning makes a substantial difference, as it comes into the picture substantially when the loan becomes nonperforming and the provisioning requirement for a secured loan (i.e., secured by eligible collateral) is substantially cheaper than an unsecured loan (i.e., not secured by a collateral). As the provisioning requirement directly hits the profit and loss accounts of the financial institution's balance sheet, the board and the management are wary of taking assets that hurt their balance sheets. Immovable collateral is generally regarded as eligible collateral by regulators, which decreases the provisioning requirements. Hence, SMEs unable to provide eligible collateral against their loan exposures are charged higher risk premiums.

Another major issue is the introduction of liquidity and leverage requirements applied to the financial sector in the aftermath of the global financial crisis. The liquidity and leverage framework demands high quality and liquid assets, as "judged" by the "market." SMEs suffer here primarily on two counts: (i) generally low external credit ratings by agencies, as noted; and (ii) an absence of flourishing capital and securitization markets in developing economies. Banks hence get penalized and may refrain from SME exposures, depending upon the credit infrastructure of the country.

In December 2017, Basel standards for the first time recognized and introduced a separate risk weight bucket (General SME Corporate 85%) for SME exposure. The risk weight recommendation is based on a study of SME risk across economies and does not require an external rating (as SMEs find the external credit rating process cumbersome and very costly) (see Box 2 for discussion of regulatory dispensation).

Box 2: Regulatory Dispensation Given for Small and Medium-Sized Enterprises

The role of regulations has always been debatable in facilitating small and medium-sized enterprise (SME) lending. With the introduction of Basel II approaches, the system of risk-weighting encourages portfolio concentrations in low-weighted assets such as government bonds, large corporates, mortgages, and lending between banks. Discussed in the subsection *Regulatory Bottlenecks in Lending to SMEs* are the adverse impacts of Basel II and Basel III regulations on SME lending. As expected, regulatory measures have been undertaken to promote SME lending, some discussed in the table below.

Measures Taken	Standard	Impact
Regulations allowed financial institutions to use collateral and collateral substitutes such as government guarantees to substitute the risk weights	Basel II	This single regulation was a major booster to credit guarantee schemes across the world. For the secured portion, the regulation allows financial institutions to substitute the covered portion with the risk-weight of the guarantor. As most of credit guarantee schemes in developing countries are backed by government, they end up attracting a 0% risk weight. For example, on an exposure of a $75,000 loan to an SME (attracting a risk weight of 75%) and a capital adequacy ratio of 8%, the capital requirement will be as follows: Unguaranteed Loan: $75,000 * 75% * 8% = $4,500. Guaranteed loan with 90% coverage: 90% * $75,000 * 0% * 8% + 10% * $75,000 * 75% * 8% = $450 (90% reduction in capital).
Concessional risk weight of 75% for SME exposure less than €1 million	Basel II	This especially helped young, micro, and small enterprises as it provides a substantial relief from an unrated risk-weight of 100%.
Size adjustment in internal rating-based approach	Basel II	For banks with internal rating-based approaches, Basel guidelines provide adjustment in the correlation formula for SMEs whose total sales or total assets are less than €50 million. This translates into lower capital requirements.
General corporate SME category introduced	Basel III	In the finalized Basel III reforms of December 2017, a new category of "general corporate SME" is introduced, where unrated SME exposure attracts a risk weight of 85%.
Size factor adjustment	CRD IV (EU)	To mitigate the adverse impact of Basel III reforms on increased capital requirements (10.5% including countercyclical buffer), the European Union (EU) advised a size factor adjustment of 0.7619 for SME exposure of up to €2.5 million (i.e., capital requirements will be adjusted to 8% or 0.7619 X 10.5%). The EU further advised a size factor adjustment of 0.85 for SME exposures exceeding €2.5 million.

A financial institution is an intermediary which connects those who save funds with those who need credit. Cost of funds is basically the sum of compensation made to the saver of funds plus a fraction of cost of operations (financial + operational). Cost of funds is determined by the business model of the bank. It is determined primarily by the funding mix of the bank and the efficiency of its asset-liability management. Profit margin is mostly determined by the market factors and, hence, predatory pricing practices are more of an issue in the financial ecosystem.

Determining risk premium is the most challenging aspect of this assessment. Broadly, this risk assessment has two cost components: the business cost associated with extending credit to a certain category of risky borrowers, and the regulatory cost (capital and provisioning) that financial institutions will incur against it. Small and medium-sized enterprises face challenges on both counts.

CRD = capital requirements directive.
Source: Authors' compilation.

Fisera et al. (2019) corroborates this, as it finds in emerging markets and developing economies, Basel III implementation had a moderately negative impact on SME access to finance.[2] They also note that SMEs in the early stages of financial inclusion could have been severely impaired than SMEs that have adopted bank credit.

Access to Finance

Financing is a key component in ensuring SME growth. However, inadequate financing is the second widely mentioned hurdles troubling SMEs and has become a key constraint against SME development in emerging markets and developing countries (International Finance Corporation 2017). The International Finance Corporation projects that 65 million firms, or 40% of formal MSMEs in developing economies have an unmet financing need of $5.2 trillion annually, which is equivalent to 1.4 times the actual share of global MSME lending. East Asia and the Pacific account for the biggest share (46%) of the total global finance gap. On average, the MSME financing gap represents 19% of individual countries' GDP. In lower middle-income and high-income countries, this indicator is 20%–21%. As shown in Figure 2, the issue is exacerbated on an enterprise level: the finance gap is 81% for microenterprises and 56% for SMEs.

Figure 2: **Small and Medium-Sized Enterprises Financing Gap**

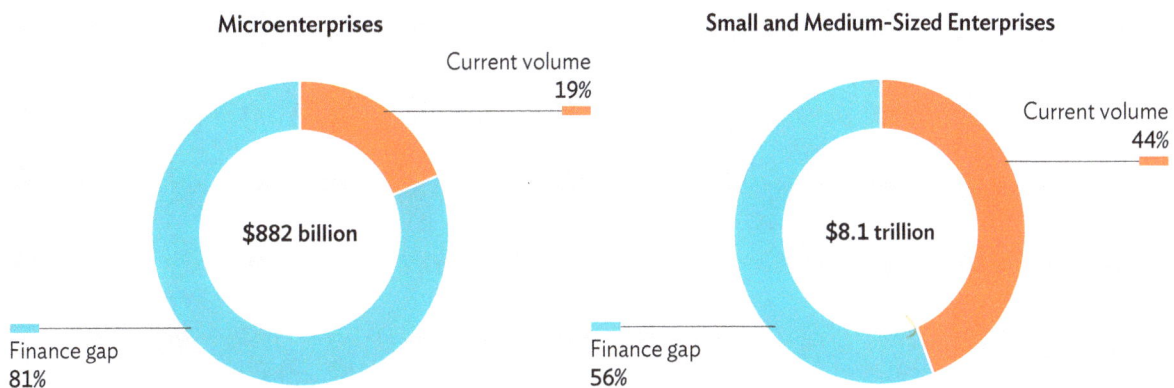

Microenterprises

Current volume 19%

$882 billion

Finance gap 81%

Small and Medium-Sized Enterprises

Current volume 44%

$8.1 trillion

Finance gap 56%

Source: International Finance Corporation. 2017. *MSME Finance Gap: Assessment of the Shortfalls and Opportunities in Financing Micro, Small, and Medium Enterprises in Emerging Markets.* https://openknowledge.worldbank.org/handle/10986/28881.

Even when the SMEs can secure finance it is often on unfavorable terms. The average interest rate billed to MSMEs on credit lines was about 170 basis points higher than that settled by large enterprises based on a survey done by the European Central Bank (ECB 2018). The public sector has tried to play multiple roles in the resolution of the financial access gap of MSMEs. Efforts have been met with varying success, but the problem persists. The next section therefore discusses underlying economic rationale and financial practices to assess the challenges SMEs face in accessing finance.

---

[2]   Basel III is the Bank for International Settlements' international regulatory framework for banks.

While institutional and structural reasons explain small and medium-sized enterprises' (SMEs) perennial issues in accessing finance, important underlying nonfinancial reasons also explain it. For policy makers, it is important to understand each country's or region's diverse set of infrastructure and constraints. A policy solution, addressing the factors discussed below, might be able to improve SME access to finance.

Asymmetric Information

Asymmetric information issues arise when parties to a transaction have different degrees and quality of information about the factors affecting transaction outcomes. SME owners have full and actual knowledge of revenue streams and growth opportunities, which is not readily available to lending firms. SMEs find it challenging to formally provide lenders with audited financial statements and well-laid-out business plans to support their credit and growth expectations (Berger and Udell 2005; Michaelas et al. 1999). This imperfect information and high transaction costs limit SME access to finance (Stiglitz and Weiss 1981). This is worsened because many SMEs operate in the informal sector and are not registered with the government or industry associations. This dearth of information makes risk averse financial institutions act more cautiously, leading to avoidance of SME lending.

Loss/Regret Aversion

The problem of asymmetric information is aggravated by the behavioral bias of humans involved in the lending process. Loss/regret aversion is one of the most common behavioral biases (Pompian 2012), in which humans are impacted more severely by negative outcomes and hence make less than "rational" choices to avoid the loss/regret outcomes. As lending to SMEs is typically believed "risky" and the lack of reliable and timely information makes it harder to assess creditworthiness, decision makers focus more on securing the loss aversion avenues, such as collateral, presence of guarantees, insurance, etc., which SMEs usually lack.

Defensive Decision-Making

This phenomenon occurs when decision makers are aware of the best decision for the firm or client yet choose the second-best option that protects him or her against the negative outcomes of such decisions. This phenomenon can be observed more in economies and institutions where the dominant nature of the financial industry is public (Artinger et al. 2018). In a public-sector-dominated financial ecosystem, while there is little personal cost for "indecision" or a "negative" decision, decision makers may face vigilance actions in case loans sanctioned turn nonperforming. Using an event-study methodology, it is found that vigilance activities emanate from decreased lending: the volume of credit deteriorates abruptly at the affected bank branch and neighboring branches. This effect is economically and statistically significant, persisting up to 2 years. Bank risk-taking also drops in the wake of a vigilance event (Banerjee et al. 2007).

Satisficing

The existing financial ecosystem in most economies is not well suited to the financing needs of SMEs—despite a continuous push from policy makers, lending processes have not evolved suitably for their needs. Typically, lending processes are hurt by a commonly occurring organizational phenomenon known as "satisficing"—combining "satisfy" and "suffice." Satisficing is a decision-making strategy that aims for a satisfactory or acceptable result rather than the optimal solution. Decision makers, instead of dedicating time, energy, and resources toward achieving an optimal solution (Fellner et al. 2009) when satisficing may focus more on the pragmatic effort when confronted with tasks such as SME lending. For example, under a CGS initiative where financial institutions are required to extend credit to SMEs, financial institutions may opt to extend loans under the CGS to existing SME clients—clients that could have originally obtained a loan—instead of excluded SME borrowers for fear of risks associated with unknown clients.

Public Goods

The role of government becomes critical for public goods. By definition, public goods are non-rival and non-excludable. Non-rival means that consumption of one entity does not diminish value for other consumers, and non-excludable means that benefit user groups are not identified specifically, and it is available for the benefit of the public in general. For SMEs, a lot of desirable credit infrastructure, such as public credit registries, collateral registries, etc., have the characteristics of public goods, but individual market participants lack incentive to initiate, store, and operate these services. As might be evident, the presence of a public credit registry solves the issue of information asymmetry to a great extent. Similarly, the presence of a collateral registry alleviates most of the concerns of the lenders highlighted above. However, without active public sector participation, the private sector has little incentive to invest in the development of such long-term public goods and, hence, these public goods are not initiated without public intervention in most economies.

Property Rights

Despite their best efforts, firms often find themselves in difficulty and have to be restructured or liquidated. Time is critical in this exercise and hence the presence of an insolvency and bankruptcy code, supported by robust legislative and legal infrastructure, is likewise crucial. This offers relief to borrowers and lenders equally. Borrowers, especially SME borrowers with less bargaining power, do not have to waste time negotiating terms of restructuring and can focus on the revival of the business, whereas lenders are also relieved as they can rely on past evidence of recovery prospects and value in case the loans turn nonperforming.

SMALL AND MEDIUM-SIZED ENTERPRISE FINANCING AND CHALLENGES IN ASIA AND PACIFIC COUNTRIES

IV

As outlined in Section III, small and medium-sized enterprises (SMEs) face major issues in accessing finance and multiple efforts have been made to address these, but the problem persists. The following paragraphs analyze the financial ecosystem in developing countries in Asia and the Pacific, challenges faced, and nonbanking financing solutions to these challenges.

Bank-Dominated Financial System

Asian economies are frequently described as having bank-dominated financial markets and underdeveloped capital markets, particularly venture capital, by researchers. For economies like Japan and the Republic of Korea, while the venture capital market is a very small portion of the overall SME financing market, it has been picking up at an encouraging pace in the past several years.[3] This indicates that banks are the backbone of financing. Although the soundness of the banking system has a higher quality since the Asian financial crisis, banks have been wary about lending to SMEs, even though such firms account for a great share of economic activity. ADB (2020a) results reveal that constrained access to bank credit is a structural dilemma. On the average, bank loans to SMEs comprise about 14.8% of a country's GDP and 16.9% of total bank lending in the region during 2010–2019, with a declining compound annual rate of 1.3% and 0.3%, respectively. Scrutinizing SME access to bank credit in regard to the income level of the countries in which they administer, bank credit extends to a greater number of SMEs (with a relatively low ratio of nonperforming loans [NPLs]) as the country's economy becomes more developed (ADB 2015). Asian SMEs are more or less inclined to apply for loans as global peers, according to ADB–OECD surveys (ADB 2014).

Despite their critical role in economies, SMEs face huge challenges in accessing finance in Asia. SMEs are competing with large firms and face many difficulties in securing formal financing—a financing gap, as noted earlier. For this reason, they are massively dependent on internal financial sources, which can hamper their development (OECD 2006; Harvie et al. 2013).[4]

---

[3] In the Republic of Korea, the size of Venture Capital Fund Investments remains small (1.7% of GDP in 2020) when compared to Outstanding Loans to Corporate SMEs (41.62% of GDP in 2020). However, the size of Outstanding Venture Capital Funds in the Republic of Korea has been constantly growing, albeit at a slow pace, from 1.11% (2017), 1.27% (2018), 1.42% (2019), and now 1.70% (2020) (KVCA 2021).

[4] Harvie et al. (2013) defines internal financial sources as loans from friends or relatives and personal savings.

Figure 3: Asia: Small and Medium-Sized Enterprise Financing Landscape

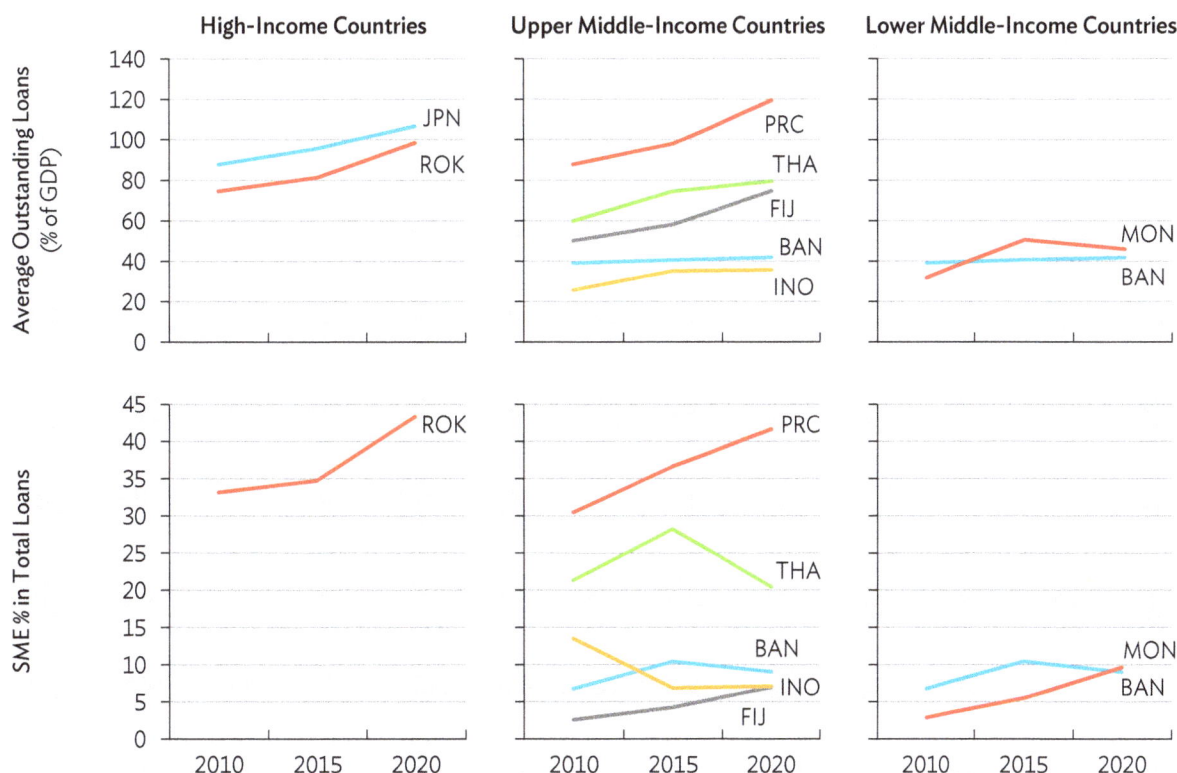

BAN = Bangladesh, FIJ = Fiji, GDP = gross domestic product, INO = Indonesia, JPN = Japan, MON = Mongolia, PRC = People's Republic of China, ROK = Republic of Korea, SMEs = small and medium-sized enterprises, THA = Thailand.

Source: International Monetary Fund. Financial Access Survey. https://data.imf.org/ (accessed 22 November 2021).

The same phenomenon is observed in a primary analysis: the IMF Financial Access Survey, 2019— for developing countries in Asia and the Pacific (Figure 3)—shows that while commercial loans as a percentage of GDP have grown, the share of SMEs as a percentage of total loans has fallen across economies. Also notable, SMEs have a higher share of commercial loans in more developed economies. Further, SMEs are more susceptible to changing market conditions as they have limited financing alternatives and lesser retained earning buffers (OECD 2015).

As noted, multiple reasons explain SMEs' difficulties accessing finance, including the following factors.

Policy Gaps

In many Asian countries, multiple public agencies are entrusted with promoting SME financing. These commonly include ministries, central banks, specially constituted bodies, etc. Sometimes, identification metrics like SME criteria, eligibility criteria, etc., are not harmonized across agencies, impacting SMEs access to finance and business prospects. For instance, in Thailand, most banks will not adopt the local definition of SMEs in their lending practice, where an enterprise is classified as an SME if it has less than 200 employees and fixed capital of lower than B200 million for production.

Instead, each financial institution adopts its definition of an SME, such as revenue lower than B500 million and/or a credit line lower than B200 million. This causes access to finance even more problematic for those SMEs that do not follow the banks' definitions. Definitions for SMEs vary across financial institutions (OECD 2005).

Vulnerability to Macroeconomic Conditions

When there is macroeconomic turmoil, financial institutions typically resort to stricter lending practices and SMEs suffer just as they need credit most. For example, OECD (2005) notes that the Asian financial crisis and the global financial crisis changed the lending behavior of Thai banks. Even as SME NPLs decreased from $3 billion (2007) to $2 billion in 2013 and total business loan NPLs decreased from 7.9% in 2007 to 3.1% in 2013, banks resorted to stricter lending practices.

Short-term loans used by SMEs increased by 179.6% over 2007–2013, whereas long-term loans increased by 35.9% over the same period. SMEs were also charged 160 basis points higher, on average, than large enterprises over 2007–2013. This difference is significant considering the SME average rate of interest was 6.7% for the period. The empirical evidence indicates that banks consider the operation of SMEs riskier than large firms, and that in a country (i.e., Thailand) with a relatively higher percentage of formal SME financing and support for the financial ecosystem (Amornkitvikai and Harvie 2016). Policy makers should take note that the post-COVID-19 world may have a similar adverse long-term impact on SME financing.

Regulatory Hurdles

SME financing has faced a lot of hurdles due to international banking regulations. Before Basel III, SMEs suffered in regulatory risk assessment. Basel II stipulated risk capital based on the external credit rating and as there was no separate risk bucket classification for SMEs, rating agencies also did not pay attention to the uniqueness of SME businesses while assessing their default risk and judged them comparably with large firms. SMEs suffered and even the best-performing SMEs may have found it difficult to get a rating higher than BBB+, which maps to a 100% risk weight. This increases the cost of capital funding for banks. Similarly, as discussed, SMEs may suffer due to the introduction of a liquidity and leverage framework in Basel III in the aftermath of the global financial crisis.

As ADB (2014) notes, there may be a negative effect on banks' lending attitudes toward SMEs in economies that have deliberately launched Basel III. These countries include the PRC, India, Indonesia, and the Republic of Korea. Even SMEs in Japan were at a disadvantage following the execution of the Basel capital accord, which has restricted their access to bank loans (Yoshino and Hirano 2011; Yoshino and Taghizadeh-Hesary 2016a). These new measures—liquidity frameworks and leverage ratio frameworks—to enhance the risk management of banks may constrain banks in granting long-term credit for enterprises and may curb the financing opportunities for SMEs, including the opening of trade finance (ADB 2015). Start-up companies are finding it more and more complex to borrow money from banks because of stringent Basel capital requirements.

V

LIMITED PRESENCE OF NONBANKING AVENUES OF FINANCE

While Asia's is a bank-dominated system, as noted, multiple avenues exist for SMEs to be financed through nonbanking financing routes. These include nonbanking financial institutions, microfinance institutions, capital markets, etc. However, the limited development and roles of such institutions greatly harms SME ability to raise finance suited to their life-stage and risk appetite.

Nonbanking Financial Institutions

While various types of nonbanking financial institutions are doing business with SMEs, they are limited in this as a percentage of overall bank loan assets in Asia. As nonbanking financial institutions cannot usually accept deposits, they operate in a more constrained environment than banks, including in avenues of raising funding and through cost; typically, they operate in a tighter asset–liability management environment. As per ADB (2020a), the nonbanking financial institution financing accounts for an average of 3.9% of GDP in Southeast Asia and 8.6% of total bank lending in the subregion during 2010–2019.

The nonbanking financial institution industry is typically small and does not specifically target SMEs. Comprehensive regulatory and policy frameworks are also lacking nationally for nonbanking financial institutions and industry performance is highly volatile and influenced by the external macroeconomic environment and bank performance.

During 2010–2019, nonbank financing has grown rapidly across Southeast Asia (except Malaysia) with an average compound annual growth of 31.8%. The nonbank finance industry, especially microfinance institutions (MFIs), has been increasing in Cambodia, the Lao People's Democratic Republic (Lao PDR), and Viet Nam.

Microfinance Institutions

In countries belonging to the lower end of the economic classification (low-income countries and low-to middle-income countries), microfinance institutions are important in financing SMEs, especially self-employed or family-run businesses. However, as the funding capacity of microfinance institutions is limited and ticket size is generally smaller for such loans, they are usually unable to cater to growing businesses or "graduated" SMEs.

Regardless, instances of success are limited in developing countries in Asia and the Pacific. For example, Cambodia, the Lao PDR, and Viet Nam, according to National Bank of Cambodia (NBC) data, MFI loans in Cambodia totaled 1.8% of GDP in 2007, rising to 26.5% in 2019, an increase of 1,402% (a compound annual growth rate of 25.3%). In the Lao PDR, MFI loans grew from KN49.2 billion ($6 million) in 2010 to KN1.3 trillion ($146 million) in 2019, an increase of 2,530%. In Viet Nam, MFI loans accounted for 0.02% in 2011 and 0.10% in 2018 of GDP.

Capital Markets

As noted, given that developing countries in Asia and the Pacific are bank-dominated, more diverse financing options could mitigate poor access to finance. Some of the advantages of financing from capital markets, especially for SMEs, include:

- **Longer tenor:** Capital market instruments offer long tenor products than the banking sector, where asset liabilities management is highly regarded. This becomes important, especially if SMEs are looking to undertake investments to grow.

- **Low cashflow pressure:** For equity financing, cashflow pressure is usually lower, as only dividends need to be paid out. It is especially advantageous during times of economic stress, as it does not impose specific repayment requirements.

- **Foreign investors:** Capital markets allow SMEs to tap foreign investors and raise funds across different growth stages of a firm.

However, despite the above advantages, SMEs typically find it challenging to access capital markets. The most common challenges faced are the:

- complications and costs involved,
- high degree of disclosure and accountability,
- corporate governance requirements, and
- dilution of control.

As such, even though many developing countries in Asia and the Pacific have taken steps to deepen capital markets for SMEs, the results have been mixed. Table 5 is a snapshot of SME exchanges in Asia and the Pacific.

The functioning of the SME capital market, as evident from Table 5, is a mixed success:

- While exchanges in the Republic of Korea, Japan, and Viet Nam have achieved significant volume (in trading and number of companies), markets in India, Malaysia, and New Zealand do not have comparable success.

- To determine the contribution of these exchanges in facilitating ease of access to finance for SMEs, trading multiples are studied (Table 5). A trading multiple is an indicator that compares the amount of trading volume to the listed market capitalization. At present, only 5 out of 11 SME exchanges have trading multiples greater than 1. This implies that even if companies are listed, they are not that actively traded. This may have adverse implications under liquidity and leverage frameworks for financial institutions under the Basel Framework.

Table 5: Snapshot of Trading Exchanges in Selected Asia and Pacific Countries

Country	Exchange	Name of Index	Trading			Number of Listed Companies
			Market Cap ($ million)	Share Traded ($ million)	Trading Multiple	
India	National Stock Exchange of India	NSE Emerge	1,820	809	0.4	188
	BSE Limited	Small and Medium Enterprises	1,613	351	0.2	222
Japan	Japan Exchange Group	JASDAQ	75,693	160,677	2.1	726
		Mothers	45,449	210,307	4.6	276
Republic of Korea	Korea Exchange	KOSDAQ	204,701	1,090,019	5.3	1,279
Malaysia	Bursa Malaysia	ACE Market	2,825	4,725	1.7	119
		LEAP Market	223	1	0.0	13
New Zealand	NZX Limited	NZAX	188	9	0.0	13
		NXT	46	0	0.0	2
Thailand	Stock Exchange of Thailand	Market for Alternative Investment (MAI)	7,368	8,769	1.2	159
Viet Nam	Hanoi Stock Exchange	Unlisted Public Company Market	38,649	2,934	0.1	250

ACE = access, certainty, efficiency; BSE = the Bombay Stock Exchange; JASDAQ = Japan Association of Securities Dealers Automated Quotation; KOSDAQ = Korean Securities Dealers Automated Quotations; LEAP = Leading Entrepreneur Accelerator Platform; NSE = the National Stock Exchange of India; NXT = NXT Market; NZAX = NZX Alternative Market, NZX = New Zealand's Exchange.

Sources: Authors; World Federation of Exchanges. 2019. *World Federation of Exchanges Annual Statistics Guide 2018*. https://www.world-exchanges.org/our-work/articles/wfe-annual-statistics-guide-volume-4.

Reforming capital markets is one of the most challenging tasks and relies heavily on the institutions of a country. The SME capital markets across developing countries in Asia and the Pacific are making progress, but with government reforms identified, it remains a long-term goal to be a viable source of alternate funding, especially in low-income and low- to middle-income countries. Although still in the onset of development, positive performance indicators for SME equity markets persist across the developing countries in Asia and the Pacific (Figure 4) (ADB 2015).

Leasing and Factoring

As part of business operations, financing, leasing, and factoring options are available to SMEs, but these are yet to be well developed in Asia, across all stages of economic development. For SMEs, multiple advantages are associated with leasing. Expenditures linked to leasing are a tax advantage, but multiple nonmonetary advantages for SMEs also exist. Leasing contracts are flexible toward customer needs (Slotty 2009), such as the option to cancel a lease before contract maturity, the possibility to renew for additional periods, options to buy the asset at termination, and so on (Chemmanur and Yan 2000). In terms of cash flow, lease payments may also be tailored to sync with SME cash flow generation. However, often due to complicated accounting requirements, SMEs face issues in leveraging this channel.

Figure 4: Snapshot of Small and Medium-Sized Enterprise Financing Market in Selected Asia and Pacific Countries (2019[a]) (%)

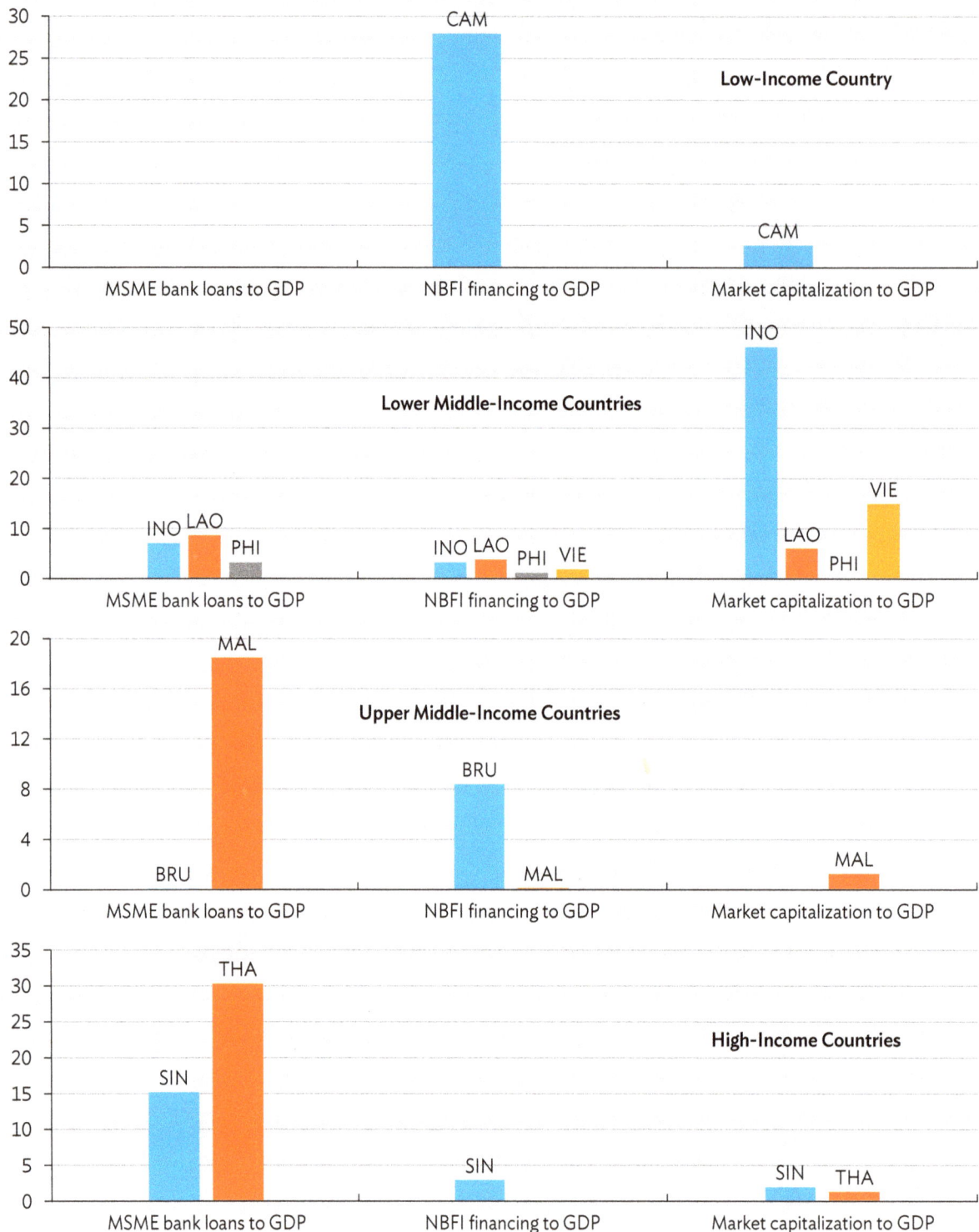

BRU = Brunei Darussalam, CAM = Cambodia, GDP = gross domestic product, INO = Indonesia, LAO = Lao People's Democratic Republic, MAL = Malaysia, MSMEs = micro, small, and medium-sized enterprises, NBFI = nonbanking financial institution, PHI = Philippines, SIN = Singapore, SMEs = small and medium-sized enterprises, THA = Thailand, VIE = Viet Nam.

[a] 2018 is the latest available data for MAL and SIN.

Source: ADB SME Monitor Volume I: Country and Regional Reviews, 2020.

Factoring is also a potent financing instrument. It allows high-risk suppliers to transfer the repayment risk to low-risk buyers. Factoring allows SMEs to promptly realize their receivables. It is also readily available for them, as factoring financing is done based on invoice-issuer credit standing and not on the SMEs. Because receivables are sold rather than collateralized, and factored receivables are not part of a bankrupt SME's estate, factoring may be particularly advantageous in nations with limited legal enforcement and a poor track record of maintaining seniority claims. However, the hurdles in technological and credit infrastructure are impediments to SMEs in accessing factoring.

One of the main hurdles for the financial industry business model is that because these operations are typically part of banks or their subsidiaries, there appears to be little or no competitive environment for these industries. Furthermore, it is not only formal debt finance that is largely inaccessible to these firms; equity markets such as initial public offering (IPO), venture capital and angel funds are also options that are not open to many small companies (Nguyen and Canh 2020). Although the reasons behind this must be thoroughly investigated, it is undeniable that providing a wider choice of financing options for SMEs will aid in national economic development (ADB 2015). A snapshot of the factoring volume in Asia and the Pacific is presented in Figure 5. The PRC, along with Australia; Japan; Taipei,China; and other economies continue to dominate the factoring landscape in the region.

Figure 5: Factoring Market in Asia and the Pacific

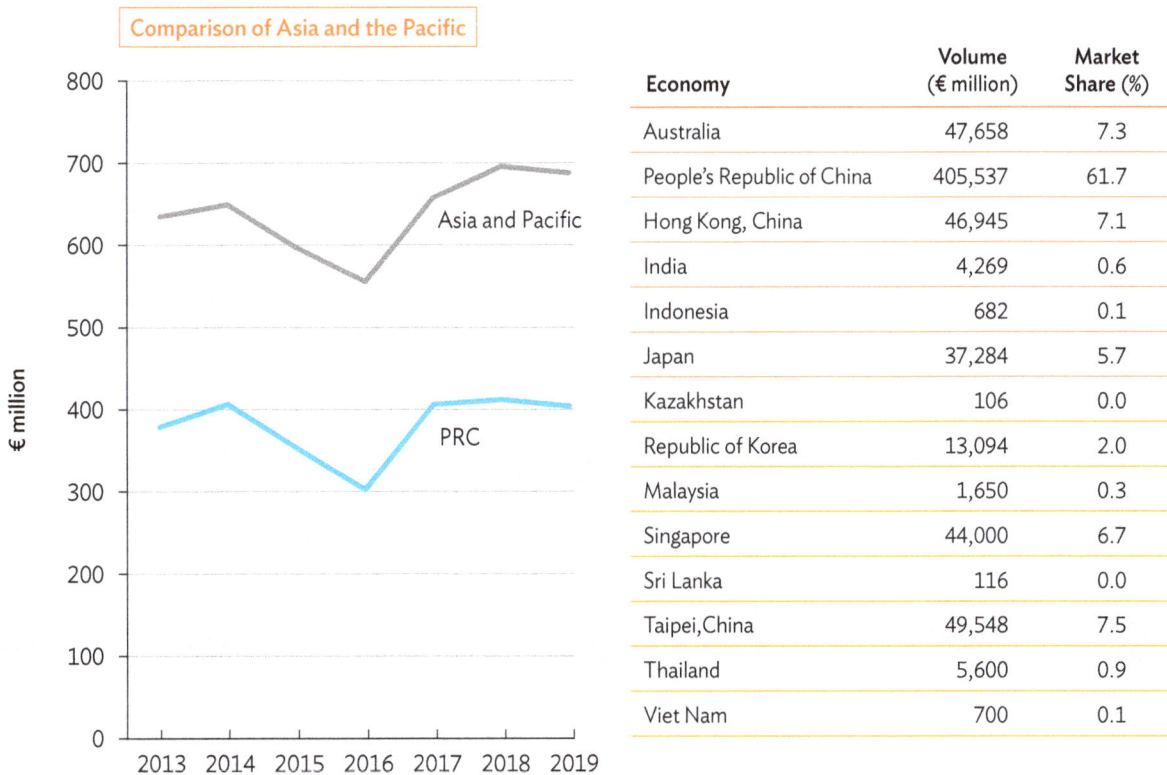

Economy	Volume (€ million)	Market Share (%)
Australia	47,658	7.3
People's Republic of China	405,537	61.7
Hong Kong, China	46,945	7.1
India	4,269	0.6
Indonesia	682	0.1
Japan	37,284	5.7
Kazakhstan	106	0.0
Republic of Korea	13,094	2.0
Malaysia	1,650	0.3
Singapore	44,000	6.7
Sri Lanka	116	0.0
Taipei,China	49,548	7.5
Thailand	5,600	0.9
Viet Nam	700	0.1

PRC = People's Republic of China.
Source: FCI. 2020. *FCI Annual Review 2020.* https://www.smefinanceforum.org/post/2020-fci-annual-review.

Alternative Credit Assessment Approach

The alternative credit assessment approach aims to accommodate SME business needs and the need for expert understanding in the credit assessment process. The approach is basically to rely on qualitative data collected on clients, often through a loan officer. This not only allows lenders to understand the strength and constraints of the SME business better, but also provides them an opportunity to accommodate SMEs to avoid punitive action using models based largely on quantitative data. This method is used to authorize loans for clients who do not have enough quantitative information, such as a credit history or financial statements. Some financial institutions also use qualitative scorecards (Berger and Udell 2004). This approach is likewise used by many fintech firms lending to SMEs in the form of "psychometric lending," in which the proprietor of the SME is asked to undertake a psychometric assessment and lending decisions are based on that by the firm. However, with the focus on automation, the last-mile loan officer role is being diminished, which may impact this form of lending in countries where this has been a significant mode of credit assessment.

To summarize, impediments to SME financing in developing countries in Asia and the Pacific stem from relatively less developed financial markets, a lack of robust and supportive credit infrastructure systems, gaps in supporting legal frameworks and quasi-judicial institutions, and a lack of innovation in lending practices. SMEs do not like cumbersome banking processes and demanding requirements. They are also not equipped to navigate complicated financial products and are highly undermined by long disbursement times.

VI CHALLENGES FACED DUE TO GAPS IN CREDIT INFRASTRUCTURE

Obtaining credit from the financial system requires reliable, timely, and robust financial information, data, and business plans. SMEs face huge challenges because of the quality and timeliness of their bookkeeping. They are often not audited externally and are prepared with a lag of 9–12 months, rendering them ineffective for financial health assessment. Further, since financial literacy is a major challenge in developing countries in Asia and the Pacific, most SMEs find preparing this documentation and dealing with financial institutions very confusing and thus tend to avoid it.

However, SMEs that passed the initial hurdles of financial illiteracy are challenged by the issue of collateral. SMEs typically lack sufficient collateral, and this has become a major impediment to the continuous growth of an SME. Even when the loan is approved after all these hurdles, SMEs usually end up paying a higher rate of interest, which affects the business position and growth potential of the firms. Box 3 summarizes SME financing impediments in Japan.

Box 3: Case Study on Small and Medium-Sized Enterprise Financing Challenges: Japan

Based on the Tankan Survey of December 2020 (Bank of Japan 2020), which compares lending attitudes of financial institutions toward small and medium-sized enterprises (SMEs) and toward large enterprises, the lines in the figure show attitudes of lending institutions toward enterprises, with a higher number indicating a more favorable attitude.

Lending Attitude to SMEs in Japan

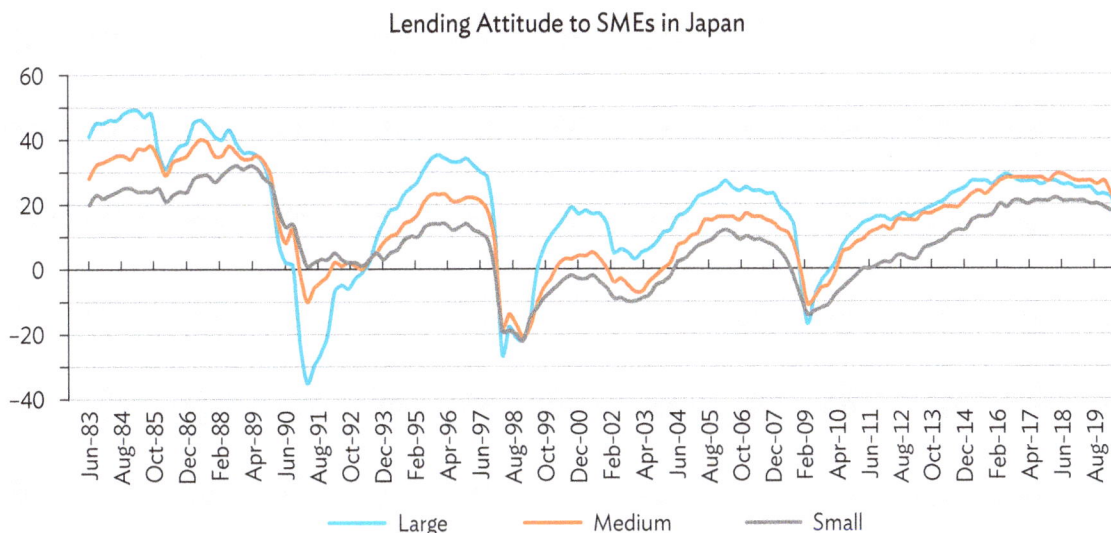

SMEs = small and medium-sized enterprises.
Source: Recomposed using data from Tankan Survey, Bank of Japan (2020).

continued on next page

Box 3: *Continued*

The Bank of Japan gives survey forms to sample firms by mail or online and administers the survey every 3 months—in March, June, September, and December. To achieve predefined standards, such as statistical correctness, the bank selects sample enterprises from the community based on industry and size classifications.

The data time series, almost 4 decades long, shows two dominant behaviors:

(i)   Over time, even though attitudes grow more favorable for all three types of enterprises, the gap between large and medium/small enterprises keeps increasing, indicating that lending institutions attitudes toward SMEs become relatively less favorable over time.

(ii)   During major crises—the Asian financial crisis or the global financial crisis—lending attitude plunges for all three kinds of enterprises and SMEs recover slowly, indicating that they continue to suffer in the post-recovery world.

These observations are for a high-income country like Japan, with an advanced, well-developed financial system and SME policies. Most of Asia does not fare well on these counts and SMEs are expected to find it tougher in those economies. The two observations are important to note given the current coronavirus disease (COVID-19) situation. Most economists have already argued that the current crisis is worse than the global financial crisis and, in the absence of the suitable policy intervention, the detrimental "sticky" effect for SMEs is going to continue much longer.

Source: Authors.

Lack of Supporting Credit Infrastructure

As discussed, in the absence of individual best-standards (accounting, governance, and businesses process systems) and assets (collateral, brand value, etc.)—as is the case with SMEs—the role of supporting credit infrastructure becomes critical in facilitating credit. Robust credit infrastructure facilitates the mitigation of prevailing information asymmetry. The supporting credit infrastructure primarily includes four mechanisms:

Credit guarantee schemes. This is one of the most common ways to support credit flow to SMEs. As noted, these schemes are common across the globe, including developing countries in Asia and the Pacific, and follow different models of funding, operations, guarantees, etc. The CGS tries to achieve financial and economic additionality and aids credit flows to SMEs by sharing the default risk with lenders. The CGS guarantees banks compensation of a certain percentage of loans taken by the SME in case of a default. The experience with the CGS has been mixed in developing countries in Asia and the Pacific, which is discussed in greater length later in the publication.

Credit registries. As noted, reliable and timely information is critical for credit assessment of SMEs. However, because most SMEs do not have robust internal accounting and governance systems and face difficulty "breaking into" the financial system, they suffer in credit assessment. The credit registry, either public or private, collates information on creditors from various institutions and allows the potential lenders to rely on such information for assessment. The information generally includes past payment history, borrowing history, etc. Most developing countries in Asia and the Pacific have credit registries, but most restrict themselves to financial information.

A successful case study in Japan is the credit risk database (CRD). The organization was established voluntarily in 2001 mainly comprising CGSs throughout Japan. It gathered extensive financial and nonfinancial data on SMEs and microenterprises to employ data to model the risk associated with MSMEs and then improve financing chances and business efficiency. With the rich data gathered over the years, the database has assumed a critical role in financial infrastructure after solidifying its position in June 2009 by becoming a limited-liability intermediate corporation—the CRD Association.

Collateral registry. A collateral registry is a record of legal claims to personal property that has been pledged as security for a loan. Lenders can use transparent collateral registries to see if the collateral being presented as a loan security has already been pledged to another lender. Similar to the credit registry, this registry keeps account of collateral offered. Absent a collateral registry, financial institutions find it difficult to possess the asset, establish the lien, avoid fake or multiple claims, etc. The collateral registry keeps unique track of the assets, eliminating these problems. However, most developing countries in Asia and the Pacific have only adopted the immovable collateral registry. SMEs typically have movable assets (as noted, vehicles, goods, machines, etc.) and banks often do not lend against such assets. The creation of a movable collateral registry makes these movable assets bankable and allows SMEs to obtain the credit against them. Asian economies that have successfully implemented such a registry include Singapore and Hong Kong, China, among others. Considering that, in a World Bank sample from 2002–2010, about 60% of firms have access to finance and 47% have a loan. Box 4 details a study of movable collateral registries.

Box 4: Impact of a Movable Collateral Registry

To reduce the issue of information asymmetry, banks typically demand collateral from small and medium-sized enterprises (SMEs). Movable assets such as machinery and equipment, inventory, etc. account for a significantly larger share of SME assets than do fixed assets, such as land or buildings. However, in developing countries, due to inadequate legal and regulatory environments and enforcement issues, banks are usually reluctant to lend against the movable collateral. Ergo, movable assets become "dead capital."

A movable collateral registry is a repository of interest in or ownership in movable assets. It solves two key issues: (i) it notifies parties about the presence of a security interest or legal contract claim, and (ii) priority of the lenders vis-à-vis third parties.

Using firm-level surveys from 73 countries, World Bank researchers looked at the impact of adopting collateral registries for movable assets on firms' access to bank funding. The impact of the introduction of movable collateral registries was observed to be economically significant: access to bank funding is increased by about 8%, while access to loans is increased by 7%, thanks to the movable collateral registry reform (see graph). These are sizeable effects.

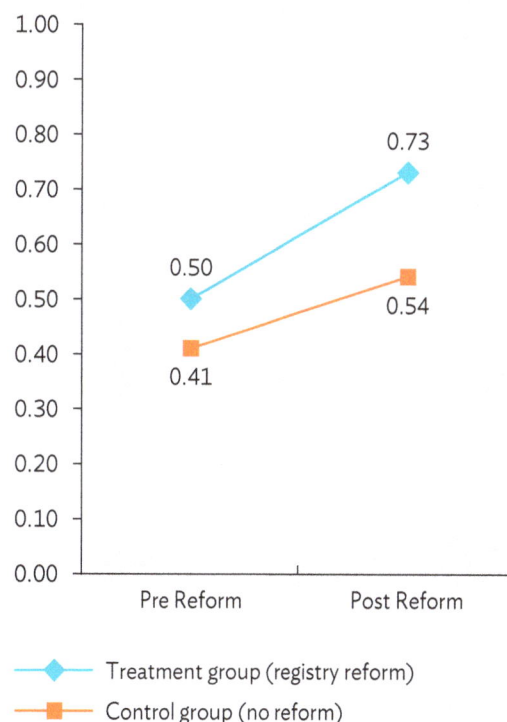

Source: I. Love et al. 2013. *Collateral Registries for Movable Assets: Does Their Introduction Spur Firms' Access to Bank Finance?* https://documents1.worldbank.org/curated/en/731881468314344960/pdf/WPS6477.pdf.

Insolvency mechanism. Despite the above systems in place and businesses' best efforts, financial difficulties require either restructuring or business liquidation. The timeliness of processes is critical as the business loses value quickly with delays (Thorburn 2000). Hence, banks, especially lacking strong credit history and collateral, desire swift resolution of insolvency. The efficiency of the insolvency mechanisms rests majorly on nonfinancial institutions, including legal frameworks and quasi-legal bodies, such as adjudication courts. Further, it needs a robust supply of quasi-financial entities, including insolvency professionals, distressed fund buyers, and price-discovery mechanisms to ensure that banks get fair assessment and pricing of assets under resolution.

In Asia, developing countries do not fare well on insolvency mechanisms, especially for small borrowers, which act as serious impediments in credit to SMEs.

A good example of this is Singapore, where, according to the Ease of Doing Business Ranking 2019 (World Bank 2019b), insolvency gets resolved in 0.8 years and lenders get 88.7 cents back on the dollar. The primary reason for faster resolution and higher rate of recovery is complete support of the laws and legal system. Singapore has progressive bankruptcy laws that were overhauled significantly in 2017 on the lines of Chapter 11 in the US Bankruptcy Code.

Singapore has a strong legal base for civil charges against liable persons or parties. For fraudulent trading, in addition to the criminal charges, the courts can declare a person responsible without limitation for the debt of the insolvent company. The track record of such prosecution is praiseworthy. The prosecuting authorities regularly charge such frauds and courts impose deterrent sentences to uphold the ethical standards of business. The recent thoroughly revamped laws passed aim to make Singapore the leading center for debt restructuring in Asia and the Pacific. The laws include, in line with Chapter 11, progressive features such as expanding courts' jurisdiction over foreign corporate debtors, automatic moratoriums on filing of applications extending to related entities, as well as rescue financing, enhanced disclosures, and establishing a dedicated bench of specialist insolvency judges, etc.

The broader underlying theme of the above mechanisms focuses on the creation of a public good when the creation of a private good is either costly or infeasible. The majority of SMEs, on a standalone basis, cannot invest to bring their operations to meet the expectations of the current credit assessment system.

Public interventions to tackle the issues small and medium-sized enterprises (SMEs) face include: (i) specialized financial institutions for SME financing, (ii) SME credit insurance schemes, and (iii) SME credit guarantee schemes (CGSs). The role of the first two is examined briefly and the role of the CGS in detail in subsequent sections.

Financial Institutions Specializing in SME Financing

Developing countries in Asia and the Pacific, in many instances, have established specialized financial institutions to channel the flow of funds to micro, small, and medium-sized enterprises (MSMEs). While some such institutions engage in direct lending, others adopt the refinancing model, in which the primary node of the disbursal of loans is financial institutions.

Shinkin banks, for example, are private deposit-taking cooperative banks specializing on regional financing of SMEs in Japan. *Shinkin* banks, like city and regional banks, are protected by deposit insurance, and they must conform to capital adequacy criteria as well as other banking regulations and supervision. *Shinkin* banks, unlike municipal or regional banks, give loans primarily to member SMEs who take advantage of the *Shinkin* banks. They can issue loans to non-member SMEs, but the percentage of such loans must be limited to 20%. They can, however, accept deposits from anyone.

Shinkin banks are typically smaller than city banks, but they are larger than credit cooperatives (*shinyokumiai*). They have contributed significantly to the overall expansion of SMEs in Japan's various areas (Hosono et al. 2006) and give 14.7% of total loans to SMEs, with funds totaling JPY128 trillion ($1.24 trillion) (Shinkin Central Bank 2015).

In the Republic of Korea, the Industrial Bank of Korea is legally mandated to have 70% SME loans in its total loan portfolio. The government provides funds to the bank to cover deficits incurred and may provide a guarantee on interest and principal payments of the bank's bonds. The Industrial Bank of Korea's expansion accelerated in the 1980s, when the government's industrial policy shifted from export-oriented larger businesses to technology-intensive SMEs. Since 1981, the Industrial Bank of Korea has offered policy loans to SMEs that manufacture and sell various intermediate commodities, such as various parts, industrial materials, and tools, to larger companies. As the country's "SME bank" and through constant expansion of corporate lending bases, especially to SMEs, it has reached 1.42 million clients out of 4 million total SMEs in the country.

One of Industrial Bank of Korea's key philosophies is that "it does not take away umbrellas when it rains." As such, it the only bank in the country that extended SME loans during the Asian financial crisis in 1997 and provided 74% of SME loans to the market during the credit card crisis in 2004.

Industrial Bank of Korea's liquidity Injection helped SMEs' access to finance. The total net increase of SME financing was $19.3 billion by all domestic banks during and after the global financial crisis. Out of these, Industrial Bank of Korea played a crucial role in financing $17.6 billion of SME loans, accounting for 91% of the total net increase in loans for SMEs (Figure 6).

Figure 6: **Trend of Small and Medium-Sized Enterprise Financing Market Share: The Republic of Korea**
(in %)

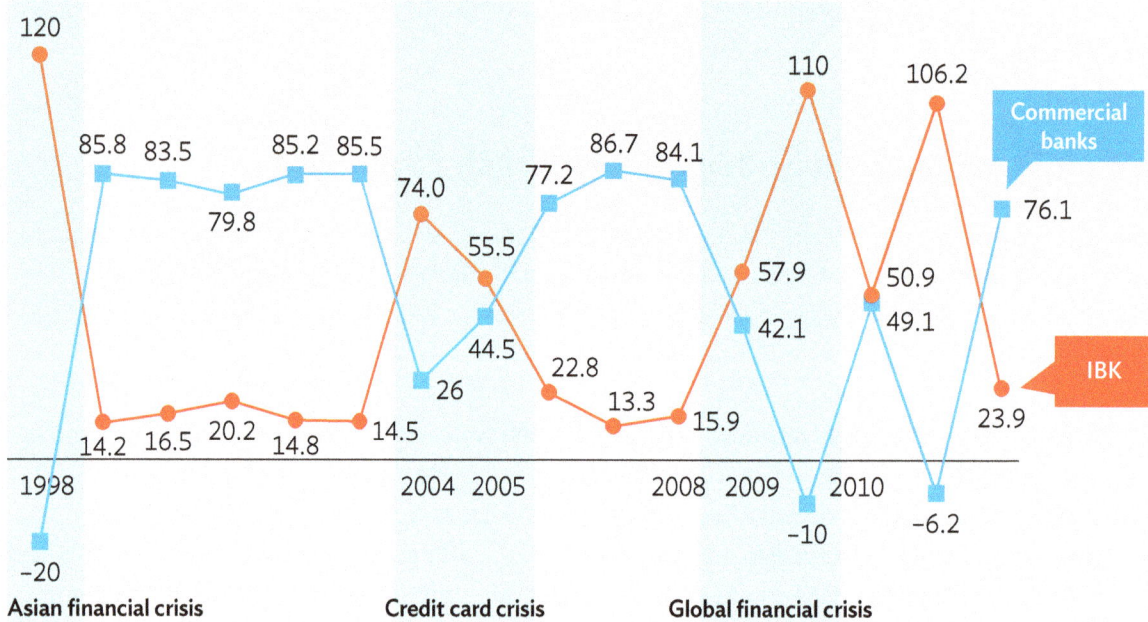

IBK = Industrial Bank of Korea.

a Market share is calculated as total small and medium-sized enterprise (SME) loans of IBK over total SME lending of the Republic of Korea.

Source: Industrial Bank of Korea. 2017. *Industrial Bank of Korea and SME Financing in Korea.* http://hts2my.newdept.com/files/occasion/cbff0f9c9fb9d5630fb874eebbbc52a7_20190730130842.pdf.

More recently, during the COVID-19 pandemic, the Industrial Bank of Korea has provided the largest amount of SME financing.

The Industrial Bank of Korea alone provided new loans for W10.3 trillion in 2015, accounting for 20% of the annual W52.8 trillion net growth in SME loans extended by all Korean banks. With a market share of 22.3% in SME loan balances, the Industrial Bank of Korea is the only Korean financial institution for SMEs with a market share of 20% or more.

In addition, as a policy bank specializing in SME lending, the Industrial Bank of Korea helped uphold the government's fiscal policy in 2015, helping to lift the country's economy out of its quagmire and stimulate the country's creative economy by launching a slew of new products aimed specifically at financing SMEs, particularly start-ups. As of the first half of 2018, unsecured loans comprised 32.3% of the SME loan portfolio and 23.6% of the micro-business portfolio of the Industrial Bank of Korea.

Meanwhile, in Thailand, the Small and Medium Enterprise Development Bank of Thailand was founded in 1964 to help SMEs start up or grow by offering loans, guarantees, venture capital, and advisory services. By the end of 2020, the bank had issued 101,520.22 million baht to 82,274 entrepreneurs (SME Development Bank of Thailand 2020).

SME Credit Insurance Schemes

SMEs need credit insurance, mainly to protect themselves in trade transactions. It becomes important as many of the risks involved in trade (political, macroeconomic, etc.) are completely outside the control of SMEs, and an issue with a major trading partner (such as political unrest), could trigger a chain of bankruptcies in SMEs in the broader economy. To protect against this, many economies operate SME trade credit insurance schemes.

Another government-owned, specialized financial institution for SME exporters is the Export-Import Bank of Thailand (EXIM Thailand). In keeping with government policies and steps to support the Thai economy, EXIM Thailand has established a number of financial services. SME start-up credit, SME Export Delight, SME border trade, SME relocation and expansion, and SME research and development and innovation credit are some of them. As per its 2019 annual report, EXIM Thailand insurance turnover stands at B121,372 million (about $4 billion), registering 31.3% annual growth (EXIM Thailand 2019).

Small, medium-sized, and large enterprises in all industries can get export credit insurance from the Sri Lanka Export Credit Insurance Corporation. Export credit insurance can help users trade with confidence in overseas markets. The insurance scheme covers political risk, country-specific risk, subsidiary risk, and others. The coverage ranges from 60%–90% of exposure.

Some countries, such as Japan and the US, also provide insurance against natural hazards. For example, the Small Business Administration in the US provides hazard insurance to cover against wind, hail, and cyclone risks. US EXIM Bank also offers up to 100% coverage for single-buyer credit insurance.

SME Credit Guarantee Schemes

Countries around the world, as noted, have been using the CGS, in various forms, as a public instrument to improve the flow of funds into targeted sectors (such as agriculture) and groups (start-ups, women, etc.). In economic terms, a public guarantee scheme is a tool that tries to close the gap between supply and demand in SME financing (Yoshino and Taghizadeh-Hesary 2016b). The CGS has existed in a number of nations since the turn of the twentieth century (Beck et al. 2010). However, more than a quarter of public CGSs were launched after the global financial crisis began in 2007.

The CGS aims to help financial sectors that are having trouble raising capital, such as SMEs. CGS participants raised their sales and survival rates in the Republic of Korea (Oh et al. 2009). France, Germany, Italy, and Spain, according to the European Association of Mutual Guarantee Societies, are the EU's largest guarantee markets by total volume.

VIII ROLE OF CREDIT GUARANTEE SCHEMES

Since a credit guarantee scheme (CGS) alone cannot deepen an underdeveloped financial system, the gaps in small and medium-sized enterprise (SME) financing that the CGS can fill should be well defined. The first and most critical step in deciding whether to set up a CGS is the need to identify its exact economic role. For this, the stepwise flowchart must be followed (Table 6).

Table 6: Identifying the Credit Guarantee Scheme Purpose

STEP 1	**Analyze access to finance issues:** "360° assessment" using industry and institutional resources to identify SMEs access to finance issues such as higher interest rates, higher rejection rates, demand for collateral, and other issues.
STEP 2	**Analyze underlying causes:** The outcome of step 1 must be analyzed to clearly identify core underlying issues. For example, higher interest rates could be due to a higher risk-weight for SME exposures, difficulty in credit assessment, or ineffective bankruptcy procedures.
STEP 3	**Analyze overlap of functions:** Assess whether the existing institutions/mechanisms have addressed, or have ineffectively addressed, the issues identified in step 2. If ineffectively addressed, reforming existing mechanisms may be considered. In all other cases, the issues may possibly be targeted with the help of a CGS.
STEP 4	**Analyze institutional market failure issues:** This step looks at market failure that requires intervention. A CGS should only target issues for which it can offer suitable, long-term, and optimal solutions. A CGS should not be a permanent solution to issues that can be solved better with mechanisms such as a movable collateral registry or a functional insolvency framework.

CGS = credit guarantee scheme, SMEs = small and medium-sized enterprises.
Source: Authors' compilation.

Further, the CGS combines a subsidy element with market-based arrangements for credit allocation, leading to less distortion in credit markets than a more direct form of intervention, such as state-owned banks. To reiterate an earlier point, the objective of the CGS is to generate financial and economic additionality.

Financial Additionality

The additionality condition measures the net-positive impact of an intervention. It means that there should be no crowding out and financing should ideally reach previously unserved/underserved SMEs. Financial additionality also includes more attractive loan size, pricing, and maturities for eligible SMEs, as well as reduced required collateral for borrowing and speedier loan processing. According to Levitsky (1997), if the CGS is effectively developed and deployed, it can generate a 30% to 35% financial additionality on average.

Economic Additionality

Like financial additionality, economic additionality is said to be generated when the SMEs supported achieve economic goals, such as increased growth, employment, innovation, or exports. It is tougher to measure than financial additionality, given the second-order effects. However, given the higher share of employment, GDP, and exports in high and upper middle-income countries than in lower middle-income and low-income countries, economic additionality is evident if the financial access to the SME improves. ADB forecasts that a 10% increase in trade finance leads to a 1% rise in employment. In many cases, this is done by relying on lenders' and SME insiders' qualitative assessments to determine whether, for example, credit availability has improved or employment have been generated (Honohan 2010).

Given these objectives, the CGS can play the following roles:

- navigating the financial system—loan advisory services
- professionalizing and scaling up businesses—business advisory services
- lack of collateral—guarantee
- poor credit assessment—loan assessor
- costly credit monitoring—loan monitoring
- poor credit information systems—maintaining a rich database
- denial of loan in risky stages—direct financing

The many CGSs in Asia and their roles are in Section X: Credit Guarantee Schemes—Examination and Country Case Studies.

How Does the Credit Guarantee Scheme Work?

As already outlined, a CGS smooths the frictions SMEs face in the lending process. Economically, in the usual case of lending to SMEs, an adverse loan supply is observable, as the backward-bending loan supply curve in Figure 7 shows. Due to information asymmetry, banks not only charge higher interest rates, but they are reluctant to lend higher amounts to SMEs "perceived" as risky. This explains the backward-bending SME loan supply curve.

However, as a CGS mitigates this information asymmetry by sharing the default risk, the expected default losses for the bank declines and those banks become more willing to lend to guaranteed SMEs. Figure 7 displays the loan supply curve with a credit guarantee system as a dashed line. The dashed line will be flatter as the CGS guarantee ratio rises, implying that SMEs will have funding easily accessible because banks will be more eager in giving them loans.

In addition to easier access, the SME gains on pricing, as pricing is related to the risk taken by the bank. As the risk is now shared by the CGS, SMEs gain favorable terms. To improve the flow of funds, the guarantee manager can also act as a loan assessor and monitor, which can help to enhance the loan quality (Zander et al. 2013).

Figure 7: Credit Guarantee Schemes and Small and Medium-Sized Enterprise Loan Supply

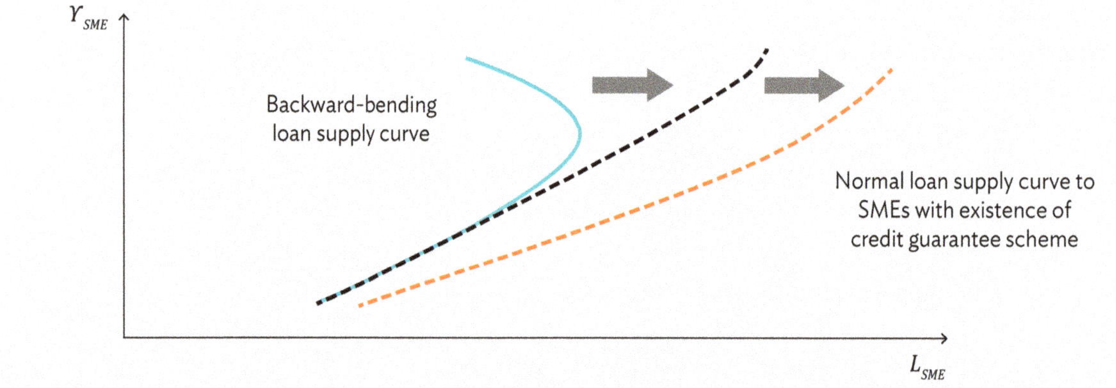

Backward-bending loan supply curve

Normal loan supply curve to SMEs with existence of credit guarantee scheme

L_{SME} = amount of loan to SMEs, SMEs = small and medium-sized enterprises, T_{SME} = lending interest rate to SMEs.

Source: N. Yoshino and F. Taghizadeh-Hesary. 2018. Optimal credit guarantee ratio for small and medium-sized enterprises' financing: Evidence from Asia. *Economic Analysis and Policy*. 62(C). pp. 342–356.

Implementation Flow of the Credit Guarantee Scheme

In a CGS, as discussed, three primary actors are involved: the borrower, financial institutions, and the CGS. As it is an ongoing relationship, these parties interact at different life-cycle stages of the loan for different purposes. Figure 8 presents a brief schematic of the flow.

Figure 8: Credit Guarantee Process Flow

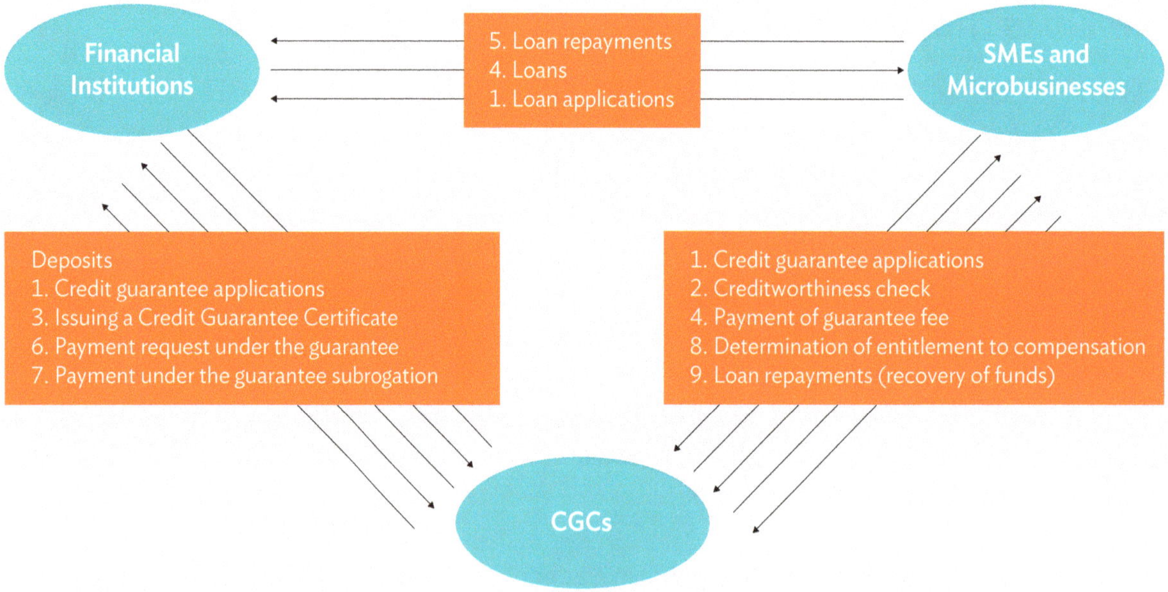

Financial Institutions

5. Loan repayments
4. Loans
1. Loan applications

SMEs and Microbusinesses

Deposits
1. Credit guarantee applications
3. Issuing a Credit Guarantee Certificate
6. Payment request under the guarantee
7. Payment under the guarantee subrogation

1. Credit guarantee applications
2. Creditworthiness check
4. Payment of guarantee fee
8. Determination of entitlement to compensation
9. Loan repayments (recovery of funds)

CGCs

CGC = Credit Guarantee Corporation, SMEs = small and medium-sized enterprises.

Source: N. Yoshino and F. Taghizadeh-Hesary. 2018. Role of Credit Guarantee Scheme and Community Based Trust Funds in SME Financing. Paper prepared for the Promoting SME Trade Finance in the CAREC Region. Xiamen. 3–4 December.

In most cases, a credit guarantee is applied through a financial institution. It is common for a guarantee agency and a financial institution to share the responsibility at a certain rate in the event of a loss in the guaranteed loan. In the case of applying for credit guarantees through such financial institutions, financial institutions can expect a decrease in the incidence of bad loans because they will improve their ability to analyze SMEs' credit. The downside is that SMEs may have less access to CGSs because financial institutions apply for guarantees by evaluating SMEs on stricter internal guidelines.

Credit Guarantee Schemes in Asia

Asia has relatively widely established CGSs: many countries in the region have schemes in some form. In 2007, Indonesia launched the People's Business Loan, a government-backed CGS for SMEs that guarantees 70% to 80% of the credit applied. The Damu Entrepreneurship Development Fund in Kazakhstan has a partial CGS for SMEs (up to 70%). The Damu Fund administers interest rate subsidies for loans to entrepreneurs and gives bank guarantees to entrepreneurs when acquiring loans. The Damu Fund covers up to 85% of the total amount of microcredit, with a maximum nominal interest rate of 6% per year for the final borrower (Damu 2017).

Since July 1972, Malaysia's Credit Guarantee Corporation Berhad has issued guarantees to SMEs. The Bank of South Pacific (a regional bank) in Papua New Guinea offers SMEs partial credit guarantees (50% of the credit applied). In the Republic of Korea, there are three public credit guarantee institutions: the Korea Credit Guarantee Fund (KODIT), the Korea Technology Credit Guarantee Fund (KOTEC), and the Korean Federation of Credit Guarantee Foundations. KODIT primarily offers guarantees to start-ups that are not focused on information technology as well as export-oriented SMEs. The fund's principal goal is to promote balanced economic development by providing credit guarantees for the liabilities of budding SMEs that have inadequate tangible collateral.

CGSs also discharge certain critical niche roles in the region:

Further lending—To extend its cooperation with the Bangko Sentral ng Pilipinas, the Development Bank of the Philippines also has a credit surety fund credit facility through which eligible cooperatives and nongovernment organizations can apply for loans, either to re-lend to their members who request financing for their businesses (wholesale) or to utilize for a cooperative's or nongovernment organization's entrepreneurial business activities directly (retail). To expand banks' lending to MSMEs, the Development Bank of the Philippines has developed the Sustainable Entrepreneurship Enhancement and Development program, Retail Lending for Micro and Small Enterprises, and the Credit Surety Fund Facility (ADB 2015).

Disaster control—Following the tsunami and earthquake tragedy in Fukushima, Japan in March 2011, the government concluded to increase credit guarantee ratios to 100% (full guarantee), as many SMEs found it problematic to obtain credit from banks (Yoshino and Taghizadeh-Hesary 2014).

In Table 7, which looks at the credit guarantee landscape, it is evident that while the CGS in Asia has been present for a long time, governance and operations models adopted by them are very different. While most countries (the Republic of Korea, Japan, etc.) have specialized central agencies to administer CGSs; countries like Sri Lanka do not.

Similarly, the nature and extent of operations is wide ranging. While most CGSs limit themselves to just extending credit guarantee services, bigger CGSs, like those in Japan, Malaysia, and others, provide a buffet of complementary services. The table, a good snapshot of the CGS landscape in Asia, suggests that the CGS in a country may evolve uniquely in response to its financial and political system.

Table 7: Credit Guarantee Landscape in Selected Asia and Pacific Economies

Economy	Institution	Established	Business Operations			Target Clients	Regulator	Net Asset ($ million)	Coverage Ratio (%)	Max. Leverage	Guarantee Fee (% avg.)
			CG	CI	Others						
India	CGTMSE	2000	✓			MSE	Government	–	50–85	–	1.00–2.00
Indonesia	Askrindo		✓	✓	Surety bond, customs bond, trade credit insurance, etc.	MSME	Regulatory Authority	371	70–80	10x net worth	1.20–1.50
	Jamkrindo		✓		Consulting services	MSME		520	70–80	10x net worth	2.28
	PKPI		✓			MSME		0.7	75	–	1.50
	Jamkrida Jatim		✓			Micro/small		5	–	–	–
	Jamkrida Bali		✓			Micro/small		–	–	–	–
Japan	JFC	2008		✓		MSME	Government and Regulatory Authority	22,093	–	–	–
	NFCGC	1953	✓			MSME			80–100	6x capital funds	0.90
Republic of Korea	KODIT	1976	✓	✓	Infra credit guarantee, consulting services, etc.	All businesses	Government and Regulatory Authority	5,693	50–85	20x capital funds	1.21
	KOREG (CGFs)	2000 (CGFs: 1996–2003)	✓		Consulting services, etc.	MSME		–	85–100	15x capital funds	1.10
	KOTEC	1989	✓		Technology appraisal and valuation, technology certificate, equity finance, M&A, technology transfer, business support, etc.	Tech-SME		–	85	20x net asset	1.26
Malaysia	CGCMB	1972	✓		Direct lending, securitization, equity financing, credit bureau services, and consulting services	MSME	Central Bank	814	50–100	6x reserve	3.65
Nepal	DCGC	1974	✓		Guarantee for savings and fixed deposits	SME/ Priority sector	Government	14	75	–	1.00

continued on next page

Table 7: *Continued*

Economy	Institution	Established	Business Operations			Target Clients	Regulator	Net Asset ($ million)	Coverage Ratio (%)	Max. Leverage	Guarantee Fee (% avg.)
			CG	CI	Others						
Papua New Guinea	SBDC	1990	✓		Business training program, consulting services, etc.	Start-up	Government	–	80	–	–
Philippines	SBC	2001 (SBGFC: 1991)	✓		Direct lending, MSME note, preferred shares, capacity building programs for SMEs and financial institutions, etc.	MSME	Central Bank	44	70–80	3x	–
Sri Lanka	Central Bank of Sri Lanka (no specialized institution)	1967	✓		Activities as a central bank	Profitable businesses	–	5	50–80	–	1.00
Thailand	TCG	1991	✓		Consulting services, etc.	SME	Government	382	–	10x equity	1.75

– = data not available, CG = credit guarantee, CGCMB = Credit Guarantee Corporation Malaysia Berhad, CGTMSE = Credit Guarantee Fund Trust for Micro and Small Enterprises, CI = credit insurance, DCGC = Deposit and Credit Guarantee Corporation, JFC = Japan Finance Corporation, KODIT = Korea Credit Guarantee Fund, KOREG = Korean Federation of Credit Guarantee Foundations, KOTEC = Korea Technology Credit Guarantee Fund, MSMEs = micro, small, and medium-sized enterprises, NFCGC = National Federation of Credit Guarantee Corporations, PKPI = Indonesian Justice and Unity Party, SBC = Small Business Corporation, SBDC = Small Business Development Corporation, SMEG = Small and Medium Enterprise Credit Guarantee Fund, SMEs = small and medium-sized enterprises, TCG = Thai Credit Guarantee Corporation.

Source: Asian Development Bank. 2014. *ADB–OECD Study on Enhancing Financial Accessibility for SMEs: Lessons from Recent Crises.* Manila.

For 2012–2019, ADB committed a total of $3.2 billion to support small and medium-sized enterprise (SME) financing operations. Over the 8-year period, the contribution to the sector grew 378%. Annual commitments generally increased up to 2017, but were subdued in the following 2 years (Table 8).

Table 8: **ADB Small and Medium-Sized Enterprise Financing Operations**

A. By Product ($ million)

| | Commitment Year | | | | | | | | |
	2012	2013	2014	2015	2016	2017	2018	2019	Total
Sovereign									
a. Loan	–	88	150	228	166	700	281	195	1,808
b. Grant	3	–	1	4	–	3	–	–	11
Nonsovereign									
c. Loan	106	181	60	65	195	75	329	330	1,340
d. Equity	1	15	–	–	–	–	–	–	16
Total (a+b+c+d)	**110**	**284**	**211**	**297**	**361**	**778**	**610**	**525**	**3,176**

B. By Region ($ million)

| | Commitment Year | | | | | | | | |
	2012	2013	2014	2015	2016	2017	2018	2019	Total
Central and West Asia	10	71	151	242	6	403	145	105	1,134
East Asia	–	138	60	–	105	100	155	180	737
Pacific	–	–	–	–	–	–	–	–	–
South Asia	100	10	–	55	250	275	110	240	1,040
Southeast Asia	–	50	–	–	–	–	200	–	250
Regional	–	15	–	–	–	–	–	–	15
Total	**110**	**284**	**211**	**297**	**361**	**778**	**610**	**525**	**3,176**

– = data not available, SMEs = small and medium-sized enterprises.

Note: Does not include technical assistance projects.

Source: Sector Advisory Service Cluster – Finance, Asian Development Bank.

ADB's support for SME financing comprises mainly sovereign and nonsovereign loans. Most of the loans extended were financial intermediation loans lent to public and private sector institutions for onward lending to SMEs. For some of the projects, targets were set for the end-beneficiaries, such as female-owned enterprises or enterprises located in rural or underdeveloped areas.

Recognizing the importance and long-lasting role of supporting credit infrastructure, ADB also helped enhance the enabling environment for SME financing through legal and regulatory reforms, strengthening of financial regulators and institutions, and establishing the necessary market infrastructure.

In terms of regions covered, for the period under review, Central and West Asia received the most allocations at 35.7%, followed by South Asia (32.7%), and East Asia (23.2%) (Figure 9).

Figure 9: **ADB's Small and Medium-Sized Enterprise Financing Operations by Region**
($ million)

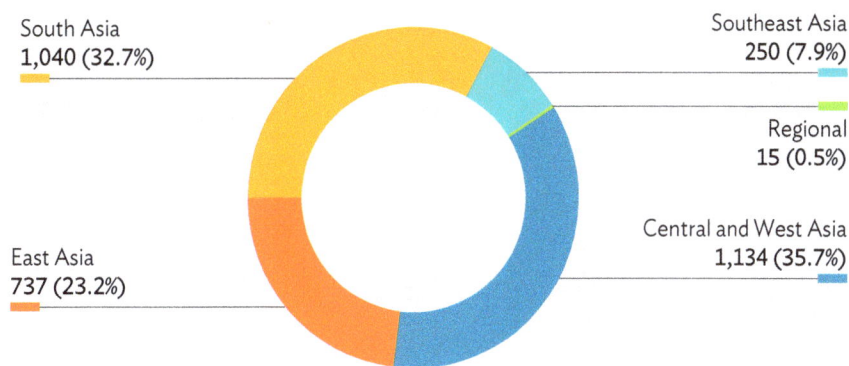

South Asia
1,040 (32.7%)

Southeast Asia
250 (7.9%)

Regional
15 (0.5%)

Central and West Asia
1,134 (35.7%)

East Asia
737 (23.2%)

Note: Does not include technical assistance projects.
Source: Authors' calculations using data from Sector Advisory Service Cluster – Finance.

ADB Support for Credit Guarantee Schemes

ADB experience suggests supporting credit guarantee schemes (CGSs) has been instrumental in providing much needed financing to Asian SMEs. The organization's support for credit guarantees has been implemented as part of broader financial sector programs that address supply and demand-side constraints relating to SME financing constraints. Its approach has been to combine policy-based loans, financial intermediation loans, and technical assistance to provide a comprehensive response covering financing gaps; inadequate regulatory, legal, and market structures; and weak institutional capacity. Table 9 summarizes ADB projects across the Asia region with an inbuilt credit guarantee component.

■ In Armenia, among the policy reforms supported by ADB's program was the adoption of a revised loan guarantee scheme by the Small and Medium Entrepreneurship Development National Center to improve outreach to female entrepreneurs and micro, small, and medium-sized enterprises (MSMEs) (ADB n.d., Armenia). The program assisted in providing 300 MSMEs, including start-ups, with guarantees amounting to $2.6 million, of which $1.3 million was issued to female entrepreneurs. The program was also instrumental in achieving economic impact in generating 2,780 new MSME loans.

Table 9: ADB's Credit Guarantee Scheme Support

	Project	Implementation Period	Amount	Number of SMEs Benefited
Armenia	Women's Entrepreneurship Support Sector Development Program	19 December 2013–17 December 2015	$2.6 million	300 MSMEs (151 were to female entrepreneurs, with a total value of $1.30 million)
People's Republic of China	Heilongjiang Green Urban and Economic Revitalization Project (49021-002)	1 April 2020–31 August 2023	$56 million	
	Air Quality Improvement in the Greater Beijing–Tianjin–Hebei Region—China National Investment and Guaranty Corporation's Green Financing Platform Project (50096-002)	14 August 2017–30 September 2022	€91.6 million	There are 11 SMEs financed by the GFP. CNY229 million has been invested in SMEs for green investment projects by the GFP.
Mongolia	Supporting the Credit Guarantee System for Economic Diversification and Employment Project	14 April 2016–31 October 2021	$60 million ($24.8 million of bank credit provided)	285 SMEs (49.5% are female-owned and 25.6% in rural areas)
Viet Nam	Second SME Development Program, Subprogram 2	26 May 2011–31 December 2011	$50.9 million	The number of approved loans that were supported by the government guarantee scheme increased from 1,164 in 2009 to 1,536 in 2015.

MSMEs = micro, small, and medium-sized enterprises; SMEs = small and medium-sized enterprises.
Source: Asian Development Bank.

- In Mongolia, ADB helped the government reform the credit guarantee system framework in the country. As of 2018, ADB's assistance to the Credit Guarantee Fund of Mongolia has led to the access of 181 firms to $14 million worth of guarantees on loans worth $24.8 million. The program has also assisted in securing 3,500 jobs, 1,300 of which are new (ADB 2019).

- In Viet Nam, ADB's SME Development Program led to the revision of the regulatory framework of the CGS in 2010 to ensure a more balanced credit risk and collateral sharing with participating commercial banks (ADB n.d., Viet Nam). These reforms have led to the growth of loans supported by CGSs.

Evaluations of the completed programs have noted several factors that affect the effectiveness of ADB's assistance. First, private sector participation needs to be enhanced. Adoption of technology by both, public and private sector can play a key role in that. For example, in Viet Nam, the introduction of web-based business registration and publication of key data and statistics can lead to greater transparency and private sector engagement. Even with regulatory and legal reforms supporting credit guarantees in place, the private sector remains apprehensive in lending to MSMEs due to the perceived risks involved (ADB 2016a). In addition, the institutional capacity of MSMEs (such as poor financial reporting systems, weak governance, and low productivity) need to be strengthened. The rapid growth of credit to an underdeveloped MSME sector resulting in the deterioration of loan portfolio quality has been raised as a regulatory concern (ADB 2018). Lastly, despite the establishment of guarantee institutions, SME access to finance remains a challenge. Reforms to address high collateral requirements, lending-deposit interest spread, and financial access costs need to be pursued (ADB 2020a).

Analysis of other Asian CGSs illustrates potential guidelines to address issues of effectiveness in previous CGS programs. Problems with private sector participation can be mitigated through developing the whole credit ecosystem. Policy makers must be ready to develop not only a rich credit information system consisting of a credit rating agency and credit database, but also the financial literacy and capacity of SME borrowers (Nadeem and Rasool 2018).

Additionally, moral hazard is among the most important challenges for the implementation of CGSs in several countries (Levitsky 1997). A full guarantee presents a moral hazard dilemma because banks are less likely to examine SMEs' operations and evaluate if they are sound before proceeding to extend loans. While there is no one-size-fits-all approach, policy makers should seek to address this issue by basing credit guarantee ratios on the financial soundness of banks and overall economic conditions (Yoshino and Taghizadeh-Hesary 2016c).

Lessons Learned from ADB Support

Armenia

The Women's Entrepreneurship Support Sector Development Program aimed to increase the role of female entrepreneurs in economic development and address the challenges that women and the MSMEs faced. ADB supported the program with technical assistance for capacity development. In the program's two components, the policy-based loan and financial intermediation loans, the first allocated budget to the Small and Medium Entrepreneurship Development National Center. This funded a loan guarantee scheme for start-ups, of which 50% would go to female entrepreneurs.

The program provided an important demonstration effect and a learning experience to other multilateral development banks, according to the project completion report. It addressed gender disparities and increased the number of new businesses established by women. The program was rated *likely sustainable*— access to finance by female entrepreneurs and MSMEs improved with the program's 151 loan guarantees amounting to $1.3 million. Its impact is demonstrated by the policy and regulatory changes and possible shift in attitude by financial institutions to MSMEs owned by women.

The SME development center issued gender-responsive loan guarantees through sex-disaggregated loan guarantee applications and approvals.

However, issues and lessons from the center were identified. The center must collect accurate data to measure output indicators that truly reflect outcomes caused by the program intervention directly targeting women. Policy reforms also need to be institutionalized to expand the financial limitations and operations to support the center.

In addition, ADB fell short in ensuring that a start-up database on MSMEs with sex-disaggregated data was established and sustained. This could have served evidence-based assessment of program achievements and developing programs that fully target the challenges faced by women's MSMEs (ADB 2019).

Viet Nam

The Small and Medium-Sized Enterprises Development Program sought to improve Viet Nam's business environment to support SME and private sector development. The program targeted four main outputs, one of which was enhancing SME access to finance through government reforms. Included in these reforms is the 2010 revisions on the CGS, which ensured a more balanced credit risk and collateral sharing with commercial banks.

While the revision of the CGS directly led to an increase in government-supported guarantee schemes from 1,164 in 2009 to 1,536 in 2015, implementing agencies and related stakeholders continue to highlight the need to facilitate financial access, as a significant number of SMEs remain without access to desired financing resources for their businesses. This issue stems considerably from the private sector's apprehensiveness toward SME financing due to the perceived risks involved (ADB 2016a).

The most significant challenge for the CGS in Viet Nam is the lack of risk sharing and cooperation with private financial institutions (Dang and Chuc 2019). Private banks lack the necessary risk involvement in the credit guarantee process as the government owns 98% of all CGS capital. Additionally, current regulations put sole responsibility for credit assessment on often inexperienced CGS staff, allowing banks to ignore supervision and debt recovery processes, and pushing risks solely onto the guarantors.

In addition, the CGS's role in enhancing SME access to finance has been compromised by new regulations ratified in 2014,[5] which applied stricter collateral requirements to SME loan applications. As a result, loans with a CGS have dramatically dropped since 2014.

The Vietnamese situation illustrates the greater need for cooperation and risk sharing among public and private stakeholders. International experience suggests that credit assessment should be passed to private bank entities. And to prevent risk shifting from banks, the CGS should establish an appropriate coverage ratio. This ratio should balance risk sharing with lender participation. Previous studies have indicated that a coverage ratio of below 50% is unacceptable for banks (Levitzky 1997).

Finally, a CGS should not forget its main mandate, and employ a more innovative approach that requires less strict conditions than commercial banks to allow more bank loans for SMEs. Establishing a credit risk database for SMEs similar to Japan's will allow CGS access to accurate information that can ease stringent capital requirements.

---

[5]   Decision 58/2013/QD-TTg indicates that enterprises must have their own capital of at least 20% of the projects guaranteed.

X CREDIT GUARANTEE SCHEMES— EXAMINATION AND COUNTRY CASE STUDIES

Beck et al. (2008), in a survey of 76 guarantee schemes across 46 countries, found that while the median age of the credit guarantee scheme (CGS) in the sample is 15 years, it rises to 27 years for high-income countries.

Table 10 shows the CGS based on the involvement of different stakeholders. While the nature of other schemes is self-explanatory in their names, mutual guarantee schemes or associations are formed by borrowers with limited access to bank loans. They are private and independent organizations, and each corporate member usually pays a capital contribution to the scheme fund. Their main strength is in a high degree of credit information on members and tight monitoring mechanisms. They are professionally run and enjoy some form of government support as re-guarantees, etc. In Table 10, the number of tick marks captures the role and involvement of the stakeholder (i.e., government, financial sector, etc.) in different types of CGS.

Table 10: Type of Credit Guarantee Scheme

Model	Government	Financial Sector	Business Industry	International Agencies	Example
Public guarantee schemes	✓✓✓	✓✓	✓	Not applicable	CGTMSE (India)
MGS	✓	✓✓	✓✓✓	Not applicable	Confidi (Italy)
PPP schemes	✓✓	✓✓✓	✓✓✓	Not applicable	CGC Berhad (Malaysia)
International schemes	✓✓	✓	✓	✓✓✓	USAID's Loan Portfolio Guarantee Scheme

CGC = Credit Guarantee Corporation, CGTMSE = Credit Guarantee Fund Trust for Micro and Small Enterprises, MGS = mutual guarantee scheme, PPP = public–private partnership, USAID = United States Agency for International Development.

Source: Authors' compilation.

Looking more deeply at the structures that govern the CGS, six countries are considered (the PRC, India, Japan, the Republic of Korea, Malaysia, and Sri Lanka), as are the US and the EU. Noteworthy features include:

Ownership and Administration

Four dominant models are available for the establishment and administration of the CGS. Mutual guarantee funds are more common in high-income nations, according to a 2008 World Bank study of 76 guarantee systems in 46 developed and developing countries. Much of the middle- and low-income countries have publicly administered funds (OECD 2009).

In our comparative case study, a similar pattern was observed for India, Japan, Sri Lanka, and the US, featuring public guarantee schemes; Malaysia and the Republic of Korea, public–private partnerships between central banks and financial institutions; and the PRC and the EU using diverse credit guarantee markets with public credit agencies, regional credit guarantee agencies, and mutual guarantee associations. Importantly, Sri Lanka has no separate established guarantee agency, but the government department and central bank act as the implementing agency of the CGS, respectively. ADB is working with the Government of Sri Lanka to establish a National Credit Guarantee Institution (ADB 2017).

Various models of administration exist. The Republic of Korea, Japan, and Malaysia have extensive staff to support CGS operations nationwide and they provide advisory services along with guarantees, including assessment services. In India, the CGS operates with a lean staff with no credit assessment services rendered.

Similarly, the Central Bank of Sri Lanka uses its own staff to run CGS services, and participating institutions have expressed multiple concerns about claim settlement, pay-out, and other issues, making the exercise not very effective. The US Small Business Administration, meanwhile, uses government resources extensively to run the CGS.

The PRC and the EU, as noted, have very diversified CGS markets. They include the participation of all stakeholders (public, financial institutions, corporates, etc.) and feature sophisticated products as well, such as re-guarantees. In these countries, governments have a major role in providing the institutional and legal frameworks and extending either direct funding or implicit or explicit counter guarantees.

Also notable, in countries such as the PRC, Japan, and the Republic of Korea, regional governments participate much more actively in running CGSs than in other countries in the sample. As local governments directly benefit through increased tax revenues, employment, and exports from the growth of SMEs in their areas, they are interested in promoting local SME financing. The three countries have a long history of strong central-local fiscal systems and fiscally strong local governments are potentially a great enabler for this model of CGS organization. These countries not only engage in extensive data collection and complement this with extensive credit assessment, they also have staff strength and organizational structure to embolden the credit guarantee system.

While governance success cannot be exclusively commented on based on whether it is a public, private, or a public–private partnership structure, it is clear that in countries where the CGSs are professional and separate agencies supported by robust governance and government SME policies, they have delivered good results. Countries which have successfully implemented this model are Japan (public) and the Republic of Korea, Malaysia (public–private partnership).

Regulation and Supervision

The regulation and supervision of credit guarantee institutions are primarily determined by the way the CGS is registered. For CGSs registered as a financial intermediary (usually nonbanking), it is most likely under the supervision of a central bank or another financial authority. For a public CGS or one running as an agency of the government, it is usually regulated by an act or executive order and supervised by ministries and government institutions.

As CGS operation can vary, control can be exercised by multiple organizations as well. For instance, KODIT (Republic of Korea), is monitored and assessed by multiple government departments, depending upon the function—the Ministry of Strategy and Finance (Budget Planning), the Financial Services Commission (Operation Supervision), and the Small and Medium Business Administration (Capital Contribution). Similarly, in Japan, while the Japan Federation of Credit Guarantee Corporations and Japan Finance Corporation are under the supervision of the Ministry of Finance and Ministry of Economy, Trade, and Industry (nationally), the 51 local credit guarantee companies are also under local government supervision. In some countries, schemes are under central bank supervision, such as CGC Berhad (a Malaysian company), etc.

Figure 10 outlines the multidimensional organizational and supervision structure of the credit supplement system in Japan.

Figure 10: Organizational Structure of Japan's Credit Supplement System

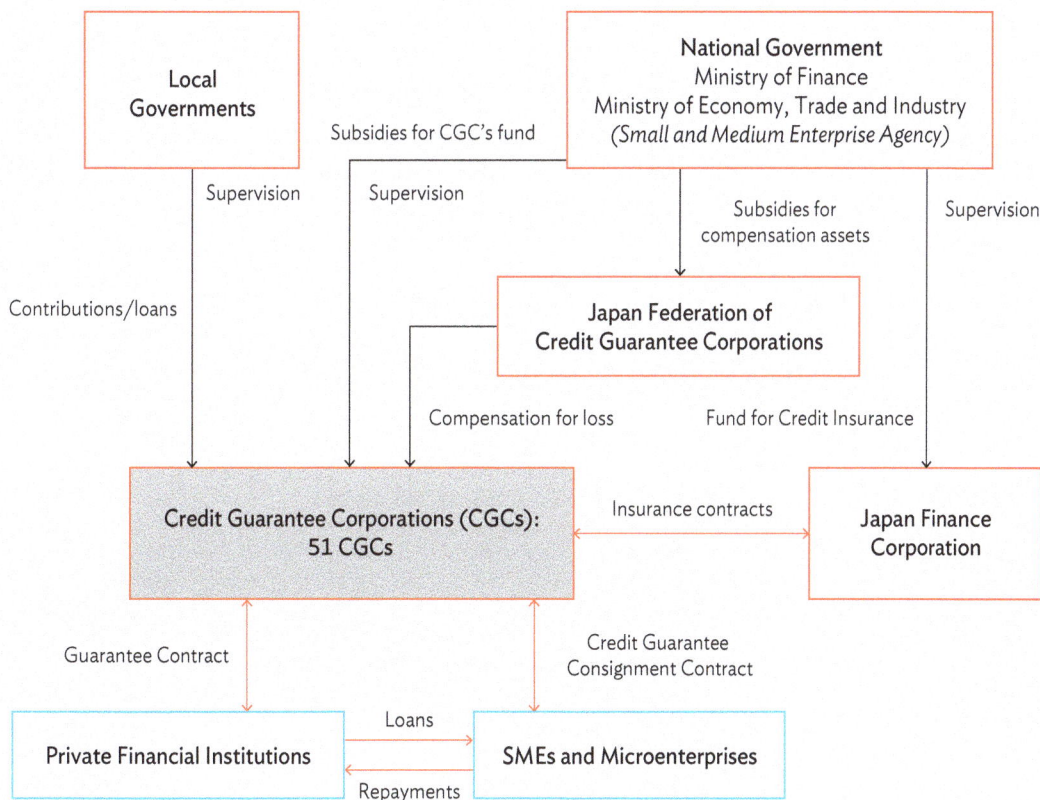

SMEs = small and medium-sized enterprises.
Source: Japan Federation of Credit Guarantee Corporations. 2014. Credit Guarantee System in Japan. Tokyo.

Services and Operations Management

Services Offered

While the primary business of CGSs is to extend guarantees, Figure 11 shows that the CGS often extends a buffet of products and services to achieve the objective. These products and services can be characterized in the following ways:

- **Financial Services**

  - **Advisory services.** The CGSs provide advisory services to SMEs to help improve book-keeping and accounting governance practices and improve timeliness of accounts preparation. Better-maintained financial recording helps SMEs secure credit as they improve the credit assessment and monitoring process for lenders.

  - **Products.** In addition to credit guarantees, depending upon the need of MSMEs, a CGS offers an array of products, such as trade credit insurance (the PRC, the Republic of Korea), refinancing of loans (EU, Sri Lanka), etc.

- **Nonfinancial Services**

  - **Business advisory services.** The CGS works with SMEs, often depending upon the growth stage of the firm (start-up, growing) to scale and capitalize their business strengths. For example, CGC Berhad in Malaysia supports and helps SMEs secure Halal certification. Similarly, in Hungary, the Rural Credit Guarantee Foundation,[6] focuses on helping SMEs from rural areas scale up their businesses.

  - **Credit assessment product.** One of the biggest challenges associated with SMEs is the availability of data and credit assessment. As such, older and established CGSs have compiled extensive databases over the years, such as the Korea Enterprise Data and Japan's CRD Association and offer an additional layer of comfort to financial institutions and SMEs by conducting credit assessment.

Figure 11: **Services from Credit Guarantee Schemes**

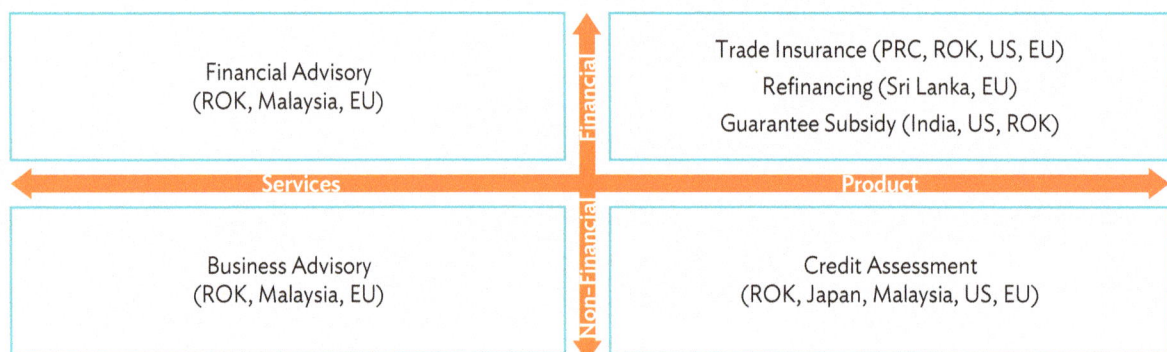

EU = European Union, PRC = People's Republic of China, ROK = Republic of Korea, US = United States.
Source: Authors' compilation.

---

[6]   See the Rural Credit Guarantee Foundation, at www.avhga.hu, for more information.

Firm Eligibility

Usually, the firm eligibility criterion of a CGS is in sync with national thresholds. In the EU and the PRC, the mutual guarantee schemes and/or private players may choose to target certain niche segments and accordingly specify their cut-off and criterion to establish eligibility for a guarantee of firms. Further, as a policy focus area, certain countries may choose to focus on SMEs belonging to a particular class (gender, race, etc.) and region. Box 5 shows the Republic of Korea's targeting of new technology-based enterprises.

Box 5: Establishing a Tech Start-Up-Focused Fund: The Republic of Korea

The Korea Technology Credit Guarantee Fund (KOTEC) was established in 1989 as a not-for-profit guarantee agency under the Korea Technology Finance Cooperation Act to provide credit guarantees to emerging technology-based firms and so modernize the economy.

KOTEC caters to technologically strong small and medium-sized enterprises to promote their growth, its support aimed at ensuring speed of innovation in these technology-related firms, which were perceived as risky.

Since its foundation, KOTEC has cumulatively provided W345 trillion in guarantees to 78,000 firms. It also provides advisory services to foster technological development and helps firms overcome obstacles.

According to the research, KOTEC has had a positive impact on the sales and productivity growth of the businesses it supports. Advisory services, review, and system-supporting technology have all led to a high loan survival rate.

Sources: J. W. Kang and A. Heshmati. 2008. Effect of credit guarantee policy on survival and performance of SMEs in Republic of Korea. *Small Business Economics*. 31. pp. 445–462; S. Roper. 2009. Credit Guarantee Schemes: a tool to promote SME growth and innovation in the MENA Region. Paper prepared for the 3rd MENA-OECD Working Group on SME Policy. Paris. 26 October.

Type of Guarantee

The type of guarantee is important in deciding the guarantee delivery model of the CGS. Two primary types of guarantees exist: retail guarantees and portfolio guarantees. Retail guarantees are usually costlier, as they involve individual assessment, and they are preferable if the guarantee-giving entity has an information advantage over lenders about the SMEs. This model is commonly observed in mutual guarantee schemes. Mutual guarantee schemes have better information on their members and, hence, can better assess credit risk than lenders.

Similarly, central CGSs in Japan, the Republic of Korea, and Malaysia have extensive information on SMEs and can assess risk better. Japan, the Republic of Korea, and Malaysia, and CGS and/or mutual guarantee schemes in the EU, offer retail credit guarantees for exposure in their credit guarantee portfolios.

The decision to offer a portfolio guarantee is not made on an individual basis. Rather, granting a guarantee is subject to a common criterion such as the loan amount, a minimum degree of trustworthiness based on financial statistics, the intended use of funds, the firm's geographic location, or its industry connection. This system usually necessitates less skill on the side of the CGS and has reduced administrative costs. Table 11 compares two types of guarantees.

Table 11: **Portfolio versus Retail Guarantees**

	Portfolio Guarantee	Retail Guarantee
Staff requirement	Low	High
Operational cost	Low	High
Risk differentiation	Comparatively less	High
Decision criterion	Predefined threshold (loan amount, tenor, sector, group, etc.)	Individual risk assessment
Suitable	New CGS	Mature CGS
Risk targeting	Low ability	Can target new risky firms such as start-ups, tech firms, etc.
Additionality	Low	High
Moral hazard	Middle	Low

CGS = credit guarantee scheme.

Source: Authors' compilation.

Risk Management Tools

Coverage Ratio

The coverage ratio is the portion of the loan that the CGS guarantees. Careful consideration is important to minimize moral hazard. Beck et al. (2010) found an average coverage ratio of 80% across 76 schemes around the world. In the European Union State Aid Framework, an upper maximum of 80% ratio is also defined as the upper limit for guarantee coverage through public funding.

Coverage can also be determined through an auction system that potentially minimizes moral hazard. Chile's FOGAPE and Mexico's National Guarantees Fund adopt the auction model to decide coverage ratio.

In our sample of case countries, the coverage ratio ranges between 50%–90%. Deciding coverage ratio is often one of the most challenging issues. In an economy with significant information asymmetry between borrower and lenders, or lenders are heavily reliant on collateral to make lending decisions, a higher coverage ratio might be required to incentivize lenders to lend to SMEs and with minimum collateral. However, policy makers should be cautious and should not set the coverage ratio too high. The coverage ratio should be set optimally to give financial institutions "skin in the game" to conduct proper due diligence and credit appraisal of the borrowers. In a few nations, the coverage ratio is used as a policy instrument to attract a specific group of small business owners, going up to 100% in limited instances to support certain categories of loans (such as technology in the Republic of Korea; micro firms in the US, etc.). Likewise, the Indian Credit Guarantee Fund Trust for Micro and Small Enterprises gives female entrepreneurs and SMEs in the country's northeast better coverage rates.

Tenor and Credit Instruments

The maturity of loans promoted by a CGS varies by country and by product. CGS-backed loans are directly related to the credit origination process set by lenders—implying that the amount and tenor of a loan is decided by use of funds and borrower's creditworthiness and contributions.

In general, credit guaranteed loans are approved and disbursed through established eligibility criteria, which are agreed between the CGS and lenders concerning the type of credit instruments—whether working capital loans and/or investment financing—that should be targeted and supported. While working capital loans supplement the day-to-day operations of a company and are crucial for maintaining solvency and employment, investment financing supports long-term initiatives such as investments in machinery and expansion projects and are crucial for long-term economic growth.

Ideally, a CGS should support all kinds of financing instruments, which has been the case in most credit guarantee institutions across the world. A survey of 60 public CGSs across 54 countries by World Bank noted that 85% of CGSs in the sample offer coverage for both instruments, in almost equal proportions (Calice 2016).[7] Similarly, surveys of CGS in Western Europe (Chatzouz et al. 2017), Central, Eastern, and South-Eastern Europe (Vienna Initiative 2014), and Middle East and North Africa (Saadani et al. 2011) illustrate similar results, with a majority of institutions providing coverage for both.

However, if a CGS must concentrate on one option due to lack of funds or risk aversion, targeting investment financing is the more ideal approach, as it creates more additionality derived from long-term SME growth and development (Green 2003). OECD (2011) notes that more focused funds, particularly where these exclude guarantees for working capital, have higher levels of additionality. Further, some CGSs choose to restrict working capital loans due to the perceived risk of non-asset backed loans (OECD 2011). The World Bank survey of public CGS reflects these theories well, as most of the remaining 15% of CGSs in the sample only provide investment finance. Banks that only promote longer-term loans include the Canada Small Business Financing Program (CSBF) in Canada, Macedonian Bank for Development Promotion in Macedonia, Caisse Centrale de Garantie (CCG) in Morocco, and Tunisian Guarantee Company (SOTUGAR) in Tunisia.

The World Bank and European Bank Coordination Initiative prescribed key principles for CGSs. These include adopting a mandate on establishing eligibility criteria for supporting different types of credit instruments—short-term working capital loans and/or long-term investment financing. While the best approach has not yet been determined, a report by KPMG establishes that a CGS should establish support for both purposes. Additionally, restrictions should be established on the size and tenor of the loans and total exposure to any single borrower or lender.

---

[7]   The scope of the survey encompasses CGSs in 22 high-income, 29 middle-income, and 3 low-income countries. By regional distribution, the survey covers 4 CGSs in Africa, 13 in Asia, 15 in Europe, 11 in the Middle East and North Africa; and 17 in North America, Latin America, and the Caribbean.

The CGS needs to strictly balance facilitating access to finance and operational sustainability. However, a CGS should not have strict conditions similar to that of a commercial bank. CGS should implement a more innovative approach that requires easier conditions than commercial banks and should alleviate high collateral requirements. For example, Lebanon's Kafalat Innovative, one of three credit guarantee activities, explicitly requires banks not to impose collateral requirements on borrowers. Rather, a 10% equity provision must be provided instead.

Pricing

The CGS makes money by charging fees for loan guarantees, which has an impact on borrower incentives. Up-front and annual fees are common, and they frequently coexist. The former has the benefit of discouraging ineligible loans and guaranteeing that early defaulting borrowers pay into the scheme. Up-front fees for the countries in the sample ranged from 0%–3.5% and annual fees are usually less than 1%.

Fee reductions are frequently offered to firms in specific target groups. For example, if a company is innovative or committed to green growth, KODIT will lower its fees by 0.1% to 0.3%. The system determines whether the fee is paid by the borrower or the lender. Beck et al. (2010) found that fees are paid by the borrower in 56% of the 76 schemes studied, while the bank covers the charge in 20% of the schemes.

In the majority of European schemes studied by the European Association of Guarantee Institutions (2012), the bank collects the charge (63%), however in 37% of cases, SMEs pay the guarantor directly, bypassing banks. OSEO in France, the German Guarantee Banks, and mutual schemes in Spain and Portugal are just a few examples.

Regardless of who is paying, the borrower has to bear the cost, directly or indirectly, unless explicitly prohibited by the regulation.

Box 6: Credit Risk Database: Japan

Japan founded the Credit Risk Database (CRD) in 2001 using government funding from the Bank of Japan and the Japan SME Agency, an authorized body of the Trade Ministry. It was established primarily to collapse of the "bubble economy" that existed from 1986–1991, in which Japan's financial institutions had been extending extensive lending on land collateral based on the presumption of perennially rising land prices. When the bubble burst in 1992 (average land prices continued to decline until 2006), a severe credit crunch ensured due to a lack of credit appraisal capacity and constraints and deterioration in credit culture.

With little collateral, small and medium-sized enterprises (SMEs) faced the worst of this, compounded as concurrent needs to fulfil Basel II implementation demanding much more sophisticated risk management practices, relying on data.

An efficient and low-cost credit risk evaluation tool was needed, specifically to promote transaction-based lending.

Features of the Credit Risk Database

The CRD collects extensive data on SMEs, including financial and nonfinancial data such as owning or not owning real estate, successor or no successor, birth year of the chief executive officer, etc., as well as default data (3 months or more arrears, bankruptcy, subrogation, etc.).

continued on next page

Box 6: *Continued*

A data cleaning exercise is done leveraging the existing database. For example, regional business statistics may be analyzed if figures of a restaurant in a Tokyo district are consistent with other restaurants, revealing cases of false data or "window dressing" in financial statements.

The CRD deploys credit risk modeling that "risk-order" the SMEs. Banking institutions can apply this risk-ordering and apply it to any sublevel analysis (industry, region, scale, etc.). The horizon of model output is typically 1–3 years, which gives financial institutions the flexibility to use it for working capital (less than 1 year) and for term loans.

Comparison with Credit Bureaus

While appearing similar to credit bureaus, the credit database is actually different and potentially could complement credit bureaus. The table compares the two.

	Credit Bureaus	**Credit Database**
Information	Personally identifiable	Anonymized information
Discipline for borrowers	Direct—acquire good financial collateral and avoid blacklisting	Indirect—move to higher credit rating group by improving business and financial information
Promoting competition in the financial market	Reduce information monopoly	Reduce estimated risk premium
Privacy and legal issues	High constraints as dealing in sensitive private information	Little to no constraint as working with anonymized information and dealing with institutional players

Source: Authors' compilation.

CRD Products and Services

- **Risk assessment of borrower.** CRD enables banks to assess the risk of SME borrowers, even if they do not have extensive financial information. CRD enables risk assessment by ascertaining their group and advising risk profile based on it. This has reduced information asymmetry greatly which allowed CGS to charge differentiated fees and financial institutions can increase collateral free lending.
- **Development and validation of internal rating models of financial institutions.** While Basel II approaches facilitate internal ratings-based models, they require long-period data to develop the default and loss models. Banks in Japan use CRD services to develop and validate SME models.
- **Management consulting support system.** This is borrower assessment and diagnostic services given by the CRD. The system allows banks to see current risk profile standings of clients and aids assessment of future potential and restructuring, as could assess the future profile of firms based on restructuring parameters.
- **Assessment of expected loss and value at risk by the Monte Carlo Method.** The CRD offers credit risk measurement tools known as C.R.I.S.P (Credit Risk Information Superior). This calculates expected loss and value at risk of the credit portfolio of a financial institution's portfolio.
- **Development of financial products.** CRD also aids the development of new financial products. In Japan, collateralized loan obligation schemes gained success as the CRD could produce reliable estimates of average risk of a portfolio. The scoring model is used to select loans, evaluate pooled assets, and assign ratings. Investors gained added comfort, in addition to the external credit rating, about the credit risk of the portfolio.

How CRD Improved the Functioning of CGS in Japan

With incorporation of the CRD, the functioning of the CGS and, by extension, access of finance to SMEs, was greatly improved. Following are the ways in which CRD helped the credit guarantee scheme (CGS):

- **Data quality.** Data provided by SMEs to the CGS are communicated to the CRD. The CRD compares the data with existing datasets and corrects discrepancies. The Bank and Credit Guarantee Corporation initiates the lending process based on the information and risk assessment received from the CRD.

continued on next page

Box 6: *Continued*

- **Use of qualitative data in risk assessment.** SMEs often have qualitative data such as ownership, age of owner, etc. The extensive dataset and assessment by the CRD allows use of this information and offers better guarantee of risk pricing.
- **Contribution to financial performance of the CGS.** As the CRD risk evaluation is highly accurate, SME defaults have been in line with CRD projections. This prevents unexpected shocks that jeopardize CGS financial well-being and thus contributes to sustainability of the scheme.
- **Better guarantee risk pricing.** One of the most notable successes is introduction of tiered guarantee fee classification. Before the CRD, a flat fee of 1.35% was charged, but with the CRD, 9 bands were introduced and the annual rate is revised based on assessed risk. This has greatly reduced adverse selection for the CGS in Japan.

Credit Guarantee Fee Rate Classification (annual rate %)

	1	2	3	4	5	6	7	8	9
Credit guarantee fee rate under Responsibility-sharing System	1.90	1.75	1.55	1.35	1,15	1.00	0.80	0.60	0.45
Credit guarantee fee rate except Responsibility-sharing System	2.20	2.00	1.80	1.60	1.35	1.10	0.90	0.70	0.50

Source: Authors' compilation.

Success Stories

- A recent SME Agency white paper (Japan SME Agency 2019) includes an intriguing analysis on how firm performance could be enhanced by shifting management from elderly to younger people.
- **Increase in collateral free loans.** An analysis by the Japan Federation of Credit Guarantee Corporation shows that, compared to 2001, where 62% of SMEs could obtain collateral free loans, that number has increased to 92% in 2014.

Source: Authors' compilation.

Financial Sustainability

Financial sustainability is a key aspect of the CGS, which has three main sources of earnings:

- guarantee fees
- investments
- miscellaneous earnings (recoveries, tax exemptions, etc.)

Earnings from Guarantee Fees

In most cases, fee income is insufficient to cover both operating costs and loan losses (Green 2003). Analyzing several recent studies on large guarantee programs, Deelen and Molenaar (2004) stated that the CGS established for developmental purposes should not prioritize financial sustainability at the expense of its primary objective. For a CGS should consider losses to be justifiable, however, there should be a maximum limit for losses set by management. Incentives for efficient management and organization can be provided by requiring schemes to generate enough income to be financially self-sufficient.

However, this strategy can lead to excessive risk-aversion on the part of the program, suggesting that only the most creditworthy enterprises receive credit guarantees. As a result, the riskier but viable SMEs that are the objective of guarantee schemes are more likely to remain without cash. This is especially true when the loan guarantee program is part of a policy to help a specific group of credit-strapped enterprises, such as start-ups, female entrepreneurs, or businesses in underserved areas.

Earnings from Investments

Earnings from investments arise from investment of a corpus fund and reserves earnings accumulated over the years. These are expected to be high for old established CGSs (and as observed) and has contributed to the financial soundness of the CGS.

Miscellaneous Earnings

A CGS also receives earnings through post-default recoveries, but these are usually not substantial. Similarly, for mutual guarantee schemes, the guarantors may be excluded from paying taxes, allowing them to completely reinvest any profits generated by the operation. The German Guarantee Banks are one example of this. Table 12 breaks down earnings for a few developing countries in Asia and the Pacific.

Table 12: **Asian Credit Guarantee Schemes Earnings**

CGS	Fee Income	Investment Income	Other Income
KODIT (Republic of Korea)	67%	17%	16%
KOTEC (Republic of Korea)	80%	9%	11%
CGC Berhad (Malaysia)	39%	48%	13%
CGTMSE (India)	60%	33%	7%

CGC = Credit Guarantee Corporation, CGTMSE = Credit Guarantee Fund Trust for Micro and Small Enterprises, KODIT = Korea Credit Guarantee Fund, KOTEC = Korea Technology Credit Guarantee Fund.

Note: 2019 data.

Sources: Authors' compilation; latest annual reports.

To assess financial sustainability, the leverage ratio is also a useful indicator for determining a CGS's financial viability. In industrialized countries with long-established schemes, leverage ratios are often greater than in emerging countries, which have less expertise in this field (OECD 2013). A higher leverage ratio may jeopardize the faith of lenders. Some CGSs also have documented leverage ratios to signal discipline to the market. KODIT has a leverage ratio of 9.8 in 2019 (threshold 20) and the Japan Federation of Credit Guarantee Corporations has a leverage ratio of 10.8 in 2019 (threshold 60). Several mutual guarantee schemes, like Socama and SIAGI in France, and German Guarantee Banks, have a consistently high ratio (over 10). This is in line with the premise that their proximity to target groups (lenders and SMEs) and long-established local reputation promote guarantee adoption. The reputation is based on the lender's ability to reduce asymmetric information between the borrower and the lender's track record with defaulted loans, which is restricted by direct risk appraisal. Requests for guarantees increase as a result of their reputation as a dependable guarantor, and the leverage ratio rises.

The question of financial sustainability is critical, especially in the case of public guarantees, because governments are typically drawn to such schemes because of the relatively small initial cash commitments compared to the potentially massive amount of credit that may be generated. However, one should remain cautious as unsustainable running of operations could contribute to unfunded sovereign contingent liabilities, which seriously damage the CGS operations.

On the other hand, the CGSs may reinvent themselves in this age of financial technology and of big data and systems. CGS usually has a treasure trove of information on SMEs and they are dealing with other stakeholders of the financial ecosystem, that is, large firms, financial institutions, etc. The CGS can provide benefits on three fronts using this rich information. First, on leveraging this extensive database—like Korea Enterprise Data, CRD—they can improve their guarantee pricing mechanisms, which will improve CGS performance and ergo the flow of credit to SMEs. Second, they can provide pricing and risk management services to the banks. They can help banks better assess the risk and validate their rating models. Third, for SMEs, they can provide consultancy services to identify the factors (geographic concentration, inventory management, etc.) contributing to the "riskiness" of the SME and help them improve and grow. These features not only improve the access to finance, health of the overall financial sector, and performance of the CGS, it can also open additional revenue streams for the CGS, which will contribute to its financial sustainability. Box 7 discusses the CGS in Sri Lanka.

Box 7: Credit Guarantee Schemes: Sri Lanka

Sri Lanka does not have any separate credit guarantee organization. The Central Bank of Sri Lanka provides credit guarantees for banks to lend to small and medium-sized enterprises (SMEs) and has been the implementing body of different credit guarantee schemes (CGSs) since 1967. The Regional Development Department of the central bank acts as an agent of the Government of Sri Lanka. Many of the schemes were mandatory and set up to promote refinance schemes operated by the central bank or other financial institutions.

History of Credit Guarantees in Sri Lanka

Sri Lanka has inherited from its colonial past a traditional British banking system based dominantly on security-based lending, rather than cash flow-oriented lending. To mitigate this, one of the first efforts was in 1967 in implementing credit guarantee schemes for cultivating loans extended by two state banks. However, the scheme was withdrawn in 1978 due to heavy default in repayments of loans in 1977–1978.

Another compelling need for the CGS arose for the SME sector after liberalization of the economy in the late 1970s. An influx of imports with recognized brand names posed survival challenges for SMEs. To prevent large-scale bankruptcies of SMEs, in April 1978, the Government of Sri Lanka put a CGS under state banks in cooperation with the Industrial Development Board.

Subsequently, in 1979, 1982, 1987, and 1994, the government tried different small and medium industries schemes with stringent loan and monitoring conditions. The conditions for the industries schemes included coverage as low as 60%, demanding a certificate of viability from lending institutions, etc.

Meanwhile, the central bank extended guarantees for three Asian Development Bank funded schemes: the Mid-Country Perennial Crops Development Project, the Smallholder Tea Development Project, and the Agriculture Rehabilitation Project loan schemes. After the Indian Ocean tsunami in 2004, the central bank launched a special *Susahana* (microfinance) scheme in August 2005 for rehabilitation of SMEs. It also tried various guarantee schemes for apparel, jewelry, buses, etc.

continued on next page

Box 7: *Continued*

Diagnosing the Performance of the Sri Lanka Credit Guarantee System

Despite multiple attempts with the CGS and trying various operational safeguards, the CGS in Sri Lanka faces challenges due to the following issues:

- **Mandatory cover.** Many of the CGSs operated to date were tied with refinance schemes. CGSs were used primarily as a tool to promote refinance schemes. While the Central Bank of Sri Lanka argued that this was to avoid adverse selection and promote sustainability, for borrowers and lenders there was no pricing advantage as refinanced loans were already on concessionary terms. It limits the "additionality" impact of CGS.
- **Loan recovery.** The central bank played no role in recovery. Like many other countries where CGS subrogates loan and pursue loans, lenders in Sri Lanka had to pursue recovery and submit with the central bank as and when they received payment. This created operational burdens for the lenders.
- **Very high number of rejection of claims.** There was frequent rejection of claim payments citing noncompliance with conditions, such as operating instructions due to:
  - ☐ delay in claim submission by lenders (i.e., within 6 months from the date of demand notice);
  - ☐ poor monitoring by financial institutions, both at the lending stage and after the loan has defaulted;
  - ☐ lack of evidence of follow up action, i.e., reports on inspections undertaken;
  - ☐ abnormal delay in serving a demand notice once a loan goes into arrears; and
  - ☐ non-exercise of prudence in credit operations, especially on project evaluation.
- **Collateral requirements.** Operating instructions insisted on obtaining collateral to avoid the moral hazard problem to the banks, which defeated the basic purpose of the CGS.
- **Strict legal action.** Post default, the central bank expected lenders to liquidate the collateral assets without any due distinction for willful and bona fide defaulters. As productive assets are often tied as collateral, and due to this requirement, there was little room to continue operating post default, and SMEs were reluctant to obtain loans.

Hence, due to mandatory charging of guarantee premiums and yet high rejections rates, the various guarantee schemes never gained much traction with lenders. The same is evident in abysmally low (less than 1) leverage ratios as follows:

Leverage of the Central Bank Credit Guarantee Schemes

Year	Equity Funds (SLRs million)	Contingent Liability (SLRs million)	Leverage Ratio
2005	4,411	4,925	1.1
2006	5,089	3,761	0.7
2007	5,990	3,179	0.5
2008	7,087	3,133	0.4

SLRs = Sri Lanka rupees.

Source: S. De Alwis and B. M. R. Basnayake. 2009. Credit Guarantee Schemes in Sri Lanka – Way Forward. *Journal for SME Development.* 14. pp. 51–82.

The CGS was not very successful, due to operational processes and restrictions. The country is undertaking steps to mitigate the challenges, building on experience. The Asian Development Bank is working with the Sri Lanka government to establish a separate institution for administrating credit guarantees—the National Credit Guarantee Institution.

Source: S. De Alwis and B. M. R. Basnayake. 2009. Credit Guarantee Schemes in Sri Lanka – Way Forward. *Journal for SME Development.* 14. pp. 51–82. https://www.yumpu.com/en/document/read/52837037/credit-guarantee-schemes-in-sri-lanka-way-forward.

Summary Comparison of Case Countries

The CGSs in the case countries have very diverse models. The CGS, just like other institutions, has evolved to respond to challenges faced by SMEs and took shape as per the institutional framework of the country. Table 13 summarizes the case countries.

Table 13: Features of Credit Guarantee Schemes

	People's Republic of China	India	Japan	Korea, Republic of	Malaysia	Sri Lanka	United States
Established	2001	2000	1953	1976	1972	1967	1953
Credit Guarantee Structure	Very complex; 6,000+ CGCs; private dominated	Two agencies; no private players	51 regional guarantee corporations; 2 central agencies	16 regional, 2 central agencies	One central agency	Central bank; no private players	Agency of Government Department
Re-Insurance of Credit Guarantee Schemes	Yes, mainly by government	No	Yes	No	No	No	No
Capital Funding	Public + private banks	Public + specialized financial institutions	Public	Public + private banks	Public + private banks	Central bank	Public
Dedicated Staff Strength	Medium	Small	Large	Large	Large	Small	Medium
Mode of Guarantee (Portfolio/Individual)	Largely individual	Largely individual	Largely individual	Largely individual	Largely individual	Largely individual	Largely portfolio
Coverage		50%–85%	80%–100%	70%–85%	50%–100%	Up to 80%	up to 90%
Interest Rate Controlled	No	No	No	No	Yes	Yes	Yes
Guarantee Fees	2%–5%	1.00%–2.00%	0.45%–2.2%	0.5%–3%	0.5%–4%	1%	2%–3.75%
Advisory Services	Yes	No	Yes	Yes	Yes	No	No
Regulatory and Supervisory Authority	Government and regulatory bodies	Government	Government	Government and regulatory bodies	Central bank	Central bank	Government

CGC = Credit Guarantee Corporation.

Source: Authors' compilation.

Financial and Economic Additionality

Assessing the financial and economic additionality of the CGS is difficult, due to data and modeling issues. However, evidence points to the additionality of the CGS. Firms must demonstrate that they have been rejected financing in the market due to a lack of collateral in some cases to be eligible. This is the case of the US Small Business Administration 7(a) Loan Program, FAMPE in Brazil, and Turkey's Credit Guarantee Fund. The additionality assessment of case countries in the sample is done in the next section, along with other examples.

XI CREDIT GUARANTEE SCHEME EFFECTS ON SMALL AND MEDIUM-SIZED ENTERPRISES

The CGS has existed for many decades and the impact assessment of the CGS relies mainly on two issues: (i) financial additionality, and (ii) economic additionality. Financial additionality is usually concerned with the bilateral relationship between SMEs (higher acceptance, higher credit, reduced collateral, low cost) and lenders (improved risk management, reduced collateral cost management). Similarly, economic conditionality refers to the positive economic impacts due to actions of the CGS. This includes the effect of guarantees on employment, investments, taxes, and economic growth.

Robustly assessing additionality is widely recognized to be difficult due to issues in establishing a counterfactual mechanism selection processes, whose value is primarily dependent on the scheme's design, provide a key difficulty in ensuring programs' additionality. The first selection method is based on the kind of businesses that are looking for guaranteed loans. Because the financial terms of guaranteed credits are often better than those of standard loan contracts, the program may appeal to borrowers with good credit who would otherwise be unable to acquire funds without the guarantee. Furthermore, the agency in charge of the program may have an incentive to give guarantees to viable enterprises, since this reduces loan losses and so improves operating results. A second mechanism that may minimize additionality occurs at the level of lending institutions, since they may have an incentive to shift regular credits to the program in order to reduce the overall risk of their outstanding credits (OECD 2013).

Important methodological restrictions and data gaps must be addressed in the econometric analysis, particularly at the firm level. The most difficult part is usually determining an appropriate control group so that enterprises that have taken out guaranteed loans can be compared to other firms (OECD 2013). The lack of appropriate data is also a key hurdle to conducting rigorous studies of CGS performance and cost-effectiveness. Additional data must be collected and made available, as well as the existing relevant data from various sources must be combined (OECD 2017).

Most studies provide the evidence of "additionality" of the CGS. Levitsky (1997) suggests that an additionality of 60% is needed to justify a CGS. However, his own study estimated that the CGS creates an average of 30%–35% financial additionality. Table 14 presents the evidence for additionality on certain key aspects.

Table 14: Evidence of Additionality

Financial Additionality		Economic Additionality	
Dimension	**Effect of CGS Intervention**	**Dimension**	**Effect of CGS Intervention**
Access to credit	■ Increase in commercial bank loans to clients who previously did not have access to credit ■ Increase of loan size.	Improvements in commercial and economic activity	■ Increase in investments of firms/sectors benefited ■ Increase in new product developed by firms benefited ■ Increase of sales in firms benefited ■ Increase in performance ratio in firms benefited ■ Increase in the number of employees
Loan conditions	■ Longer repayment period ■ Lower interest rate	Improvement in income and quality of life	■ Increase in entrepreneurs' income ■ Increase in employees' income
Relationship	■ Reduction in collateral demand by bank ■ More rapid loan processing ■ Improved borrower graduations	Improvement in welfare	■ Increase in tax income

Source: P. Leone and G. A. Vento. 2012. *Credit guarantee institutions and SME finance.* London: Palgrave Macmillan.

Financial Additionality—Credit

Financial additionality often takes the shape of better conditions in obtaining credit for SMEs, such as higher loan volumes, lower interest rates, or a longer loan maturity, as empirical research reveals.
The evidence suggesting an increase in the number of loan recipients and, in particular, improved access to capital for new entrepreneurs or firms in innovative areas is less compelling (OECD 2013).

Similarly, a survey by KPMG (2011) shows how different CGSs enable credit to the companies whose application for credit would have been rejected if they had not been given a guarantee by the CGS.
A snapshot of various schemes showing the percent of enterprises whose application would have been rejected without a CGS guarantee support are as follows:

■ 90% (according to Fundes' estimates on Bolivia, Chile, Colombia, Costa Rica, Guatemala, and Panama);

■ 63% (according to Boocock and Shariff's estimates on 32 guarantee beneficiaries in Malaysia);

■ 48% and 68% (according to Nera's and Pieda's estimates, respectively, in the United Kingdom [UK]); and

■ 53% (according to estimates on Japanese SMEs), etc.

Most of the studies find evidence of financial additionality. The compilation in Table 15 lists the studies done to assess and establish the impact.

Measuring financial additionality is challenging because not many CGSs deployed assess this impact.
Usually, a CGS takes the measures of outreach (number of firms, percent of firms) and amount (guarantee outstanding, loan is given), and so on, as a proxy of financial additionality in their assessment.

Table 15: **Summary of Studies Establishing Financial Additionality—Credit**

Country	Author	Sample	Result
Chile	Larraín and Quiroz (2006)	700 granted firms	Credit guarantees can lead to additional credit and economic improvement in micro-small enterprises; a 14% increase in credit volume, 6% additional loans, and a 6% increase in business turnover.
	Cowan et al. (2015)	Approximately 100,000 insured loans between January 2003 and September 2006	Credit guarantees were revealed to enhance the total amount of credit; in particular, one additional dollar of guarantees boosts total credit for SMEs by $0.65.
Germany	Valentin and Henschel (2013)	–	68% additional loans, 68% more regular information, 49% additional information, 43% more intensive lending relation.
	Neuberger and Räthke-Döppner (2008)	–	50% additional loans, 23% higher loan volume, 9% lower loan rates, 16% higher loan volume, and lower loan rates.
Italy	Busetta and Presbiterio (2008)	866 firms, 1,978 guarantee contracts	Reduction in the cost of credit and more rapid banking selection process.
	De Blasio et al. (2017)	Dataset from e CERVED and Credit Register information, 2005 to 2012	Bank loans to businesses have improved as a result of the program.
	D'Ignazio and Menon (2013)	9,000 firms, 2003–2010	Significant increase in the long-term component. Furthermore, targeted firms benefited from a substantial decrease in interest rates.
Japan	Uesugi et al. (2006)	1,344 guarantee user firms and 2,144 non-user firms.	Program participants significantly increased their leverage, especially their use of long-term loans, and except for high-risk firms, become more efficient.
United Kingdom	Cowling (2010)	27,331 individual loan contracts	Reduction of credit constraints for small firms.
	Allinson et al. (2013)	1,399 businesses were surveyed including 500 EFG supported businesses and 899 unassisted businesses, 2009	EFG accounted for roughly 3% of the SME term loan market in 2009, but this has since dropped to around 1%–2%.
United States	Brash and Gallagher (2008)	8,477 firms granted in 1999–2001	Increased access to credit and lower interest rates.

– = data not available, SMEs = small and medium-sized enterprises.
Source: Authors, from respective sources.

KODIT (Republic of Korea), being one of the world's better managed CGSs has released the following measures of financial additionality:

- **Additional credit:** On average, 63% of additional credit was supplied by CGS.
- **Lower interest rate:** SMEs pay lower interest rates (3.1%, 2012) than credit loans.

A similar analysis is conducted to see if there is a visible trend in the SME interest spread compared to loans availed by all firms. A clear decreasing trend has been observed for the four countries from our case sample (Figure 12).

Figure 12: **Small and Medium-Sized Enterprise Interest Spread**

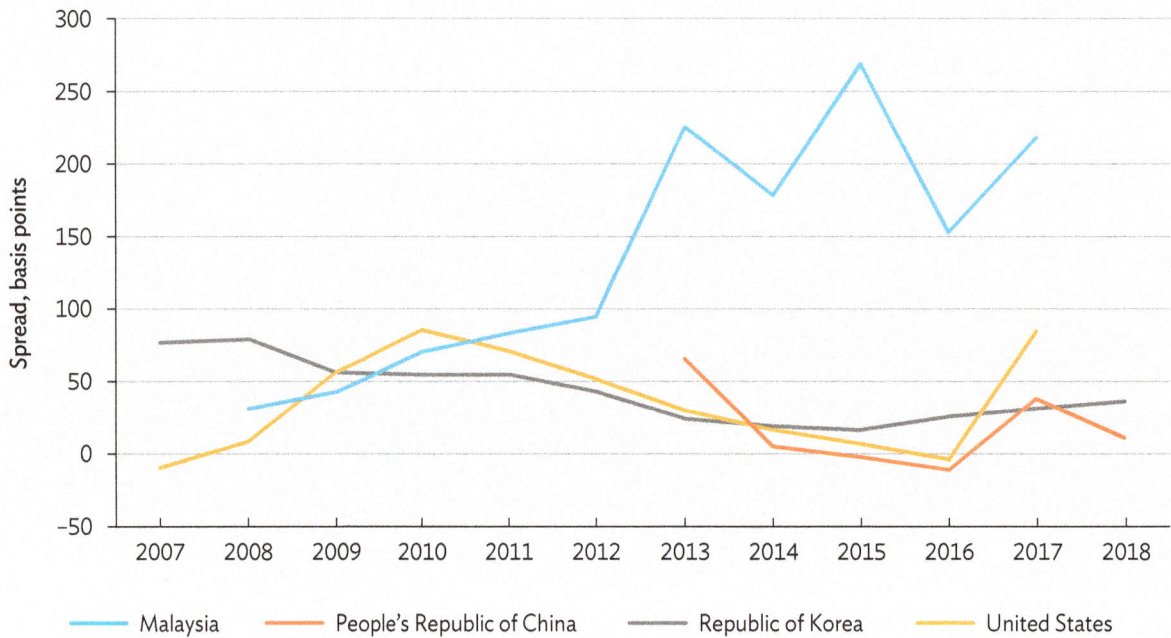

SMEs = small and medium-sized enterprises.

Note: SME interest spread computed as average interest rate (SMEs)—average interest rate (large enterprises).

Source: Authors' calculation using data from the Organisation for Economic Co-operation and Development. https://www.oecd-ilibrary.org/ (accessed April 2021).

Economic Additionality—Production/Growth

Measuring economic additionality has proven particularly difficult due to difficulties in generating the counterfactual and firm-level data, and evidence is rather limited (OECD 2013). Governments use public funds to support CGSs, as they are convinced of the potential gain for the entire economy. Accordingly, there are fewer studies on the topic, due to difficulty in the data required and accurately identifying any real effects. Table 16 lists some studies that establish the effect of CGS.

As is evident, a clear case exists for economic additionality for achieving improvement in production and/or growth. However, policy makers should not solely rely on these results, as the achievement of economic additionality depends a lot on country-specific factors and the CGSs should themselves assess the economic additionality of their policies.

Table 16: **Production and/or Growth Economic Additionality Effect of the Credit Guarantee Scheme**

Country	Author	Sample	Result
Belgium, Denmark, Finland, Italy, Luxembourg, the Netherlands, Norway, and Sweden	Bertoni et al. (2019)	174,107 loans to SMEs	Guaranteed loans have a beneficial impact on asset growth, sales, employment, and the proportion of intangible assets.
Chile	Benavente et al. (2006)	84,640 firms and 141,260 loans, 2000–2005	Firms assisted by FOGAPE increased their sales and profits after 5 years.
Germany	Neuberger and Räthke-Döppner (2008)	–	61% additional sales
Italy	Caselli et al. (2019)	38,000 SMEs	During the economic downturn, the Central Guarantee Fund increased the profitability of guaranteed businesses.
Japan	Uesugi et al. (2006)	1,344 granted firms and 2,144 non-user firms	Return on assets of program users increased more than non-users. Program users resulted in significant improvements in efficiency.
Republic of Korea	Oh et al. (2009)	95,000 to 109,000 plants, 2000–2003	Credit guarantees increased firm growth in terms of sales and employment, wages, and the survival rate of treated firms.
	Kang and Heshmati (2008)	200,702 applicants	Higher sales and productivity growth
	Liang et al. (2017)	14 banks, 2001–2010	They concluded that increasing the percentage of credit guarantees can improve cost efficiency. This demonstrates that the Republic of Korea's credit guarantee system can effectively share SMEs' credit risk in order to assist banks become more efficient.
Spain	Martín-García and Santor (2021)	2,934 SMEs	4% increase in sales
Turkey	Akcigit et al. (2021)	The sample includes around 52% of CGF-supported enterprises and 88% of CGF-backed loans.	Firms backed by the CGF were able to boost employment by 17%, increase sales by 70%, and lower their credit default risk by 0.6 percentage point.
United Kingdom	Allinson et al. (2013)	1,399 businesses were surveyed including 500 EFG supported businesses and 899 unassisted businesses, 2009	EFG has aided firms in expanding and sustaining economic activity during the challenging economic conditions of 2009–2012.

– = data not available, CGF = credit guarantee fund, EFG = Enterprise Finance Guarantee, FOGAPE = El Fondo de Garantía para el Pequeño Empresario, SMEs = small and medium-sized enterprises.

Source: Authors, from respective sources.

Economic Additionality—Employment

Employment generated is linked to SME growth. As financing is one of the biggest impediments in SME growth, it is expected that with improved access to finance, there will be a positive impact on employment. The studies validate this across the globe. Riding and Haines (2001) estimate that around 66,000 new jobs were produced in 1995 as a result of the Canadian Small Business Financing Program.

Those who participated in the program created an average of 1.53 jobs, but firms that did not participate created only 0.16 jobs (OECD 2009). Craig et al. (2007) discover that in US districts that receive more guaranteed loans, employment rates are higher. Such investigations are summarized in Table 17.

Table 17: Employment Economic Additionality Effect of the Credit Guarantee Scheme

Country	Author	Sample	Result
Belgium, Denmark, Finland, Italy, Luxembourg, the Netherlands, Norway, and Sweden	Bertoni et al. (2019)	174,107 loans to SMEs	Guaranteed loans have a beneficial impact on asset growth, sales, employment, and the proportion of intangible assets.
Canada	Riding and Haines (2001)	682 granted firms and 850,000-firm control group	Extremely efficient means of job creation, with very low estimated costs per job.
Malaysia	Boocock and Shariff (2005)	92 borrowers (data from questionnaire) + 15 case studies	The case-study firms outperformed the SME sector on employment growth. Positive and significant correlation with the average annual level of employment in a local market.
Turkey	Akcigit et al. (2021)	The sample includes around 52% of credit guarantee fund (CGF)-supported enterprises and 88% of CGF-backed loans.	Firms backed by the credit guarantee fund were able to boost employment by 17%, increase sales by 70%, and lower their credit default risk by 0.6 percentage point.
United Kingdom	Allinson et al. (2013)	1,399 businesses were surveyed including 500 EFG supported businesses and 899 unassisted businesses, 2009	Up to the beginning of 2012, the scheme had created and saved 18,800 new employment from enterprises that had taken out an EFG loan in 2009.
United States	Armstrong et al. (2010)	57,442 firms	High correlation between employment creation and level of granted loans, especially in less financially developed markets.
	Bradshaw (2002)	1,166 firms received 1,515 loan guarantees during 1990–1996	Employment increased more in firms receiving loan guarantees than among all firms.
	Brown and Earle (2017)	All 7(a) and 504 loans guaranteed by the SBA, 1992–2009	They found that each million-dollar loan provided under the SBA program resulted in the creation of 3–3.5 jobs on average.
	Craig et al. (2007)	320,000 loans, 1991–2001	The employment rate is higher in United States districts that receive more guaranteed loans.
	Hancock et al. (2007)	Granted firms under loan guarantee program and a sample of banks, 1990–2000	Guaranteed loans raised economic growth rates, employment, wages and salaries, and incomes of nonfarm proprietors.

EFG = Enterprise Finance Guarantee, SBA = United States Small Business Administration, SMEs = small and medium-sized enterprises.
Source: Authors, from respective sources.

Economic Additionality—Impact on Other Variables

In addition to production and employment, the CGS has a long-term positive effect on economic variables such as tax revenue, GDP, and factor productivity. While studies to assess such impact are difficult, Table 18 presents some.

Table 18: Economic Additionality Effect of the Credit Guarantee Scheme

Variable	Country	Author	Sample	Result
Tax revenue	Malaysia	Boocock and Shariff (2005)	92 borrowers (data from questionnaire) + 15 case studies	State tax revenues increased.
	United States	Bradshaw (2002)	1,166 firms received 1,515 loan guarantees during 1990–1996	State tax revenues increased well more than the amounts spent by the state on the program.
GDP	Germany	Schmidt and van Elkan (2010)	1,908 firms, 128 banks	Increasing investment. Direct and indirect positive effects on other economic aggregates: public net financial surplus, GDP, tax revenue, and social security.
		Hennecke et al. (2017)	–	The economic benefits of the guarantee banks are considerable due to increased production and employment. Real GDP increases by about €1.2 per euro guarantee each year. In the years 2008 to 2014, there were net fiscal gains of several €100 million in the respective federal states.
Factor productivity	Belgium, Denmark, Finland, Luxembourg, Italy, the Netherlands, Norway, and Sweden	Bertoni et al. (2019)	174,107 loans to SMEs	Guaranteed loans have a beneficial impact on asset growth, sales, employment, and the proportion of intangible assets.

– = data not available, GDP = gross domestic product, SMEs = small and medium-sized enterprises.
Source: Authors, from respective sources.

SME Credit Guarantee Financing Impact on the Financial Sector

Despite multiple positive impacts, as evident from the above discussion, one of the major areas of concern is the impact of the CGS on the financial sector. The ideal expectation is that the presence of a CGS would lead to financial deepening. However, the presence of a CGS could result in moral-hazard behavior in borrowers and lenders and credit substitution (i.e., giving less risky loans under guaranteed portfolios to reduce their risk by financial institutions). In the extreme case of banks shifting their entire loan portfolio under the program, financial additionality would be zero. While some economies (EU, US) deploy a checklist to assess the latter by requiring a financial additionality checklist, such norms are not common. The following studies have assessed this impact.

In the UK, to tackle the issue of credit rationing, the government installed the Small Firms Loan Guarantee scheme in 1981. Cowling (2010) finds evidence that access to debt finance to SMEs increased, and hence the scheme alleviated the credit rationing constraints on these businesses, at least in a general sense.

Wilcox and Yasuda (2008), for example, find that Japan's guarantee program has the potential to deepen the financial industry. Without increasing banks' loss-given-defaults, the guarantee program significantly increased non-guaranteed and guaranteed business loans. Large "city banks" increased their lending to both small and large clients. The volume of non-guaranteed bank loans to SMEs expanded three times faster than guaranteed bank loans to SMEs. Similarly, Wilcox and Yasuda show that guaranteed SME loans have increased more than guaranteed large corporate loans.

Between 1990 and 2014, Yildirim et al. (2015) investigate the efficiency of the KGF in easing the financing operations of Turkish SMEs. They discover that the KGF has increased commercial loans since 2006, and that increased investments mirror the increase in commercial loans. In other words, through promoting more investment, the KGF has been successful in boosting Turkey's capital stock.

Not only do CGS enhance financial deepening it also has the benefit of increasing bank cost efficiency. A study by Liang et al. (2017) illustrated the effects of the Republic of Korea's SME lending and CGS during 2001–2010 on participating banks' cost efficiency. Results illustrated that such schemes improve efficiency as it assures the security of loans and shares the credit risk with the bank. Not only does it help the lack of collateral of SMEs to obtain loans, but also increases the recovery rate of loans and effectively reduces a bank's cost inefficiency.

However, the impact of the CGS is not always positive. Multiple instances indicate that given borrower's moral hazard and/or lenders substitution of guaranteed loans with creditworthy non-guaranteed loans it defeats the purpose of a scheme. According to Uesugi et al. (2010), Japanese banks took advantage of the eased loan guarantee terms during the Asian financial crisis, transferring their loan portfolio under guarantee schemes.

The UK Department for International Development (DFID 2005), meanwhile, studies evidence from Chile, Egypt, India, and Poland to assess the contribution of the CGS to financial sector deepening (i.e., growth in non-guaranteed lending). It finds that the CGS inculcated positive and sustainable changes in lenders' behavior and had significant positive impact on financial sector deepening. However, the positive impact was visible in situations where certain specific factors for success were present. This means that the CGS serves as an accelerator, not driver, of financial sector deepening and CGS existence alone cannot be a sufficient condition for financial sector deepening. The study also emphasizes the critical impact of certain macroeconomic variables, such as a competitive banking environment, a monetary and regulatory framework that encourages SMEs to borrow, and a dynamic business sector. The study calls for active participation of all stakeholders (financial institutions, government, CGS, corporates) to deepen the financial sector.

The coverage ratio of many guarantee schemes in developed countries, as well as several developing countries, is 100%. However, moral hazard is high in these situations, especially if borrowers are not subject to any penalties if they default. A 100% guarantee, as seen in Canada, the Netherlands, and Lithuania, encourages strategic defaults. Especially when used in new schemes and in an environment where financial markets are still developing (ADB 2016b).

Hence, with multiple such instances, the evidence for financial sector deepening is mixed for CGSs. The key takeaway for policy makers is that one should be vigilant against the moral-hazard effect of borrowers and lenders and the portfolio-substitution effect by lenders. Also, it is important to holistically assess the financial infrastructure of a country and devise the features of the CGS accordingly.

XII THE ROLE OF CREDIT GUARANTEE SCHEMES IN PAST CRISES

Credit guarantee schemes (CGSs) are an important public policy institution. During crises, the government needs to quickly provide relief to business without compromising prudence. Authorities often use a CGS to reach needy borrowers. This strategy is also advantageous, as extending financial relief through a credit guarantee mechanism does not require immediate credit outflow and may provide the government an opportunity to smooth cash-flow over the years. In line with expectations, early evidence from many countries during the global financial crisis (2008–2009) and the uncertain recovery (2010–2011) suggests that the CGS can be an effective countercyclical tool to support lending and restore a sustainable level of financing for credit-constrained SMEs during times of increased credit market tightness (OECD 2010b).

During crisis, it becomes important to support SMEs as they start losing avenues of finance quickly from all sides. SMEs find it difficult to survive crises, particularly as:

- it is more difficult for them to downsize as they are already small;
- they are individually less diversified in their economic activities;
- they have a weaker financial structure (i.e., lower capitalization);
- they have a lower or no credit rating;
- they are heavily dependent on credit; and
- they have fewer financing options (OECD 2009).

Figure 13 shows that the interest rate spread of small loans substantially increased during crisis, underscoring the need for prompt intervention to alleviate financing concerns.

Past Policy Responses

Many countries respond to crisis by expanding existing coverage, reducing guarantee fees, and relaxing eligibility requirements, including paperwork. The Republic of Korea expanded its existing program by increasing the ceiling on individual guarantees from W3 billion to W10 billion. The coverage ratio was increased from 85% to 100% (for KOTEC, KODIT, and the local credit guarantee foundations). Changes were made to credit assessment requirements, implementing standardized ratings (A, B, C, D). Japan offered up to 100% coverage and a longer-term limit for special credit guarantee facilities.

Figure 13: **Trend of Interest Rate Spread of Small Loans**
(Monthly Data August 2007–January 2009)

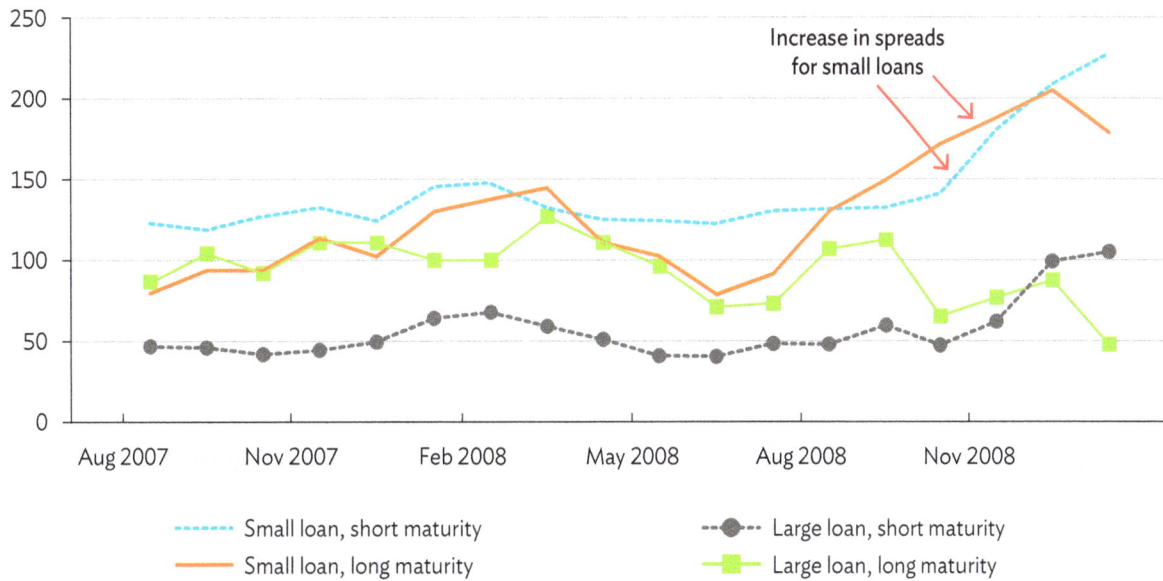

Source: European Central Bank. Monetary Financial Institutions Interest Rate (MIR) Statistics. https://sdw.ecb.europa.eu/.

Many CGSs reduce/remove required fees during economic and financial crises. Some programs, such as those in Finland, Hungary, and other EU nations, as well as the US Small Business Administration, temporarily reduced or suspended guarantee fees in 2008–2009. Other programs, such as Malaysia's SME Assistance Guarantee Scheme, did not levy a guarantee fee. The cost of a guarantee can be reduced or eliminated, providing instant financial relief to SMEs.

As per an assessment done by the European Association of Mutual Guarantee Societies of its member mutual guarantee schemes in 2009, anti-crisis guarantees given to 120,000 SMEs helped them to gain crucial access to finance, which helped those SMEs maintain operations (AECM 2010). KPMG (2011) believes that without the guarantee backing, 80% to 90% of SMEs would not have been able to receive finance, based on a survey of nine big guarantee schemes in Europe and Asia. Uesugi et al. (2010) state that 19 OECD countries used a CGS to help SMEs easily access finance and overcome financial crises.

During the COVID-19 pandemic, CGS have emerged as an effective policy tool in addressing the liquidity gaps caused by policies that mitigated the spread of the virus (e.g., social distancing and lockdowns). The low budgetary implications of CGS led many economies across the developed and developing spectrum to implement such policies. Across the European Union, almost two-thirds of EBRD countries implement this scheme and this includes countries such as Germany, France, and Portugal have leveraged these schemes to support SMEs during the pandemic (EBRD 2020). In developing Asia, economies have also expanded the use of credit guarantees to support working capital requirements of MSMEs. These include countries such as Bangladesh, Indonesia, Malaysia, and the Republic of Korea (ADB, forthcoming).

Lapses in the Guarantee Programs

According to a KPMG survey in 2011 of 9 large guarantee players[8] in Europe and Asia, guarantee schemes that supported SMEs during crisis reported a considerable increase in bad debts. In 2011, 50% of mutual guarantee schemes in Italy registered net losses (Schena 2012). In Spain, the default rate for mutual guarantee schemes increased from 6.09% in 2007 to 12.68% in 2009 and the default rate for banks increased from 2.76% to 8.50% and from 2.89% to 9.10% for savings banks (*cajas*) during the crisis. Hence, for mutual schemes, which are more exposed to risk in light of their activity, the relative increase in default was smaller than for other financial institutions (Afi and CERGAS 2010).

The government made underwriting choices under Japan's Special Credit Guarantee Program, which was implemented in 1998 during the country's banking crisis (while also providing a full guarantee). It used a shortlist of unfavorable qualities in its borrowers' screening process, such as tax delinquencies and previous bank loan defaults. The Special Credit Guarantee Program usually accepted any applicant who lacked one of the mentioned traits, resulting in an extremely high acceptance rate. This restricted credit examination, however, has been criticized as contributing to borrowers' misuse (Uesugi and Sakai 2005). Government engagement in underwriting may result in high program administrative expenses, as the Republic of Korea Credit Guarantee Fund appears to have done (Honohan 2010).

In a study of funds extended under the Special Credit Guarantee Program, it was found that borrowers misused funds by making stock investments, filing bankruptcy in less than 1 month, and availed loans just because they were easily available. Furthermore, there were instances of corruption, as government officials were arrested on the charges of receiving commission from ineligible borrowers in exchange for extending loans. These problems emerged as a result of financial institutions and credit guarantee companies performing insufficient credit checks (Uesugi and Sakai 2005). The financial cost of the guarantee program, which is borne as a result of the borrowers' default, is not insignificant. Yearly corporate debt repayments have fluctuated between JPY0.8 trillion and JPY1.2 trillion over the last 5 years, whereas annual deficits have hovered between JPY0.2 trillion and JPY0.6 trillion.

Safeguards Adopted in the Past and Current Crisis

During past crises, cognizant of moral hazard, some countries adopted interesting initiatives. During the global financial crisis, Thailand's Thai Credit Guarantee Corporation was founded to give complete guarantee coverage of 100% to increase SMEs' access to finance. However, the relaxed coverage came with the condition that participating bank's portfolio of guaranteed loans should have NPLs less than 16% of the guaranteed loans under the scheme.

---

[8]   The study by KPMG (2011) covers OSEO (France), Garantiqa (Hungary), Perum Jamkrindo (Indonesia), Eurofidi (Italy), CGC Tokyo (Japan), KODIT (Republic of Korea), SGR Valenciana (Spain), Small Business Credit Guarantee Corporation (SBCGC) (Thailand), and Credit Guarantee Fund (Turkey). KPMG. 2011. Credit access guarantees: a public asset between State and Market. https://assets.kpmg/content/dam/kpmg/pdf/2013/06/KPMG-Credit-access-guarantees-public-asset-between-State-Market.pdf.

Similarly, countries adopted many initiatives during the global financial crisis to ensure the maximum impact of CGS interventions. In the United Kingdom, the Enterprise Finance Guarantee required borrowers to show that they had previously been denied a loan outside of the program in order to ensure that the SME credit guarantee program benefited only the most vulnerable borrowers. Programs in Brazil, Turkey, and the US had similar features (OECD 2013). To eliminate zombie or unprofitable firms, only SMEs that had been profitable for the preceding 3 years were eligible for the Greek Credit Guarantee Fund for Small and Very Small Enterprises (OECD 2009).

Similar mechanisms have also been implemented by CGS that have been active during the COVID-19 pandemic. To emphasis its role in securing liquidity concerns of affected SMEs and industries, many have placed additional eligibility schemes to assure that lending activity will benefit the vulnerable SMEs. For example, in Bulgaria, firms must prove a decrease in revenue, reductions in employees, or closed production facilities. In Turkey support is contingent on the firm not cutting employment registered prior to the pandemic (EBRD 2020).

There is also an interesting example of guarantee schemes working with the financial sector. Greece established the Credit Guarantee Fund for Small and Very Small Enterprises in response to the global financial crisis (TEMPME S.A.). In addition to extending guaranteed loans between December 2008 and April 2009 under the guarantee schemes, as discussed above, TEMPME S.A. fully subsidized the cost of financing these guaranteed loans, releasing the interest burden of borrowers. In the second phase of the program after April 2009, the guaranteed loans under these schemes were given at a subsided interest rate based on negotiations between TEMPME S.A. and the banking sector, which was lower than the going market rate. The interest rate agreed was at EURIBOR + 2.10% and the loan under this scheme could exceed 30% of the average turnover of the last three accounting periods and could not exceed €350,000.

CREDIT GUARANTEE SCHEME RESPONSE TO THE COVID-19 CRISIS

The COVID-19 crisis has impacted the world severely, especially the SME sector. As seen in the past, small and medium-sized enterprises (SMEs) were the most susceptible segment, facing adversity in delayed receivables, poor business terms, lack of reserves, and avenues of financing and mounting costs. Building upon learning from the past, governments across the globe have taken proactive measures to support the SME sector. The measures varied, including credit guarantee support, direct lending, tax relief, employment support, direct transfers, etc. Figure 14 presents measures taken in Asia and the Pacific to support the SME sector.

Figure 14: **Measures to Support Small and Medium-Sized Enterprises**

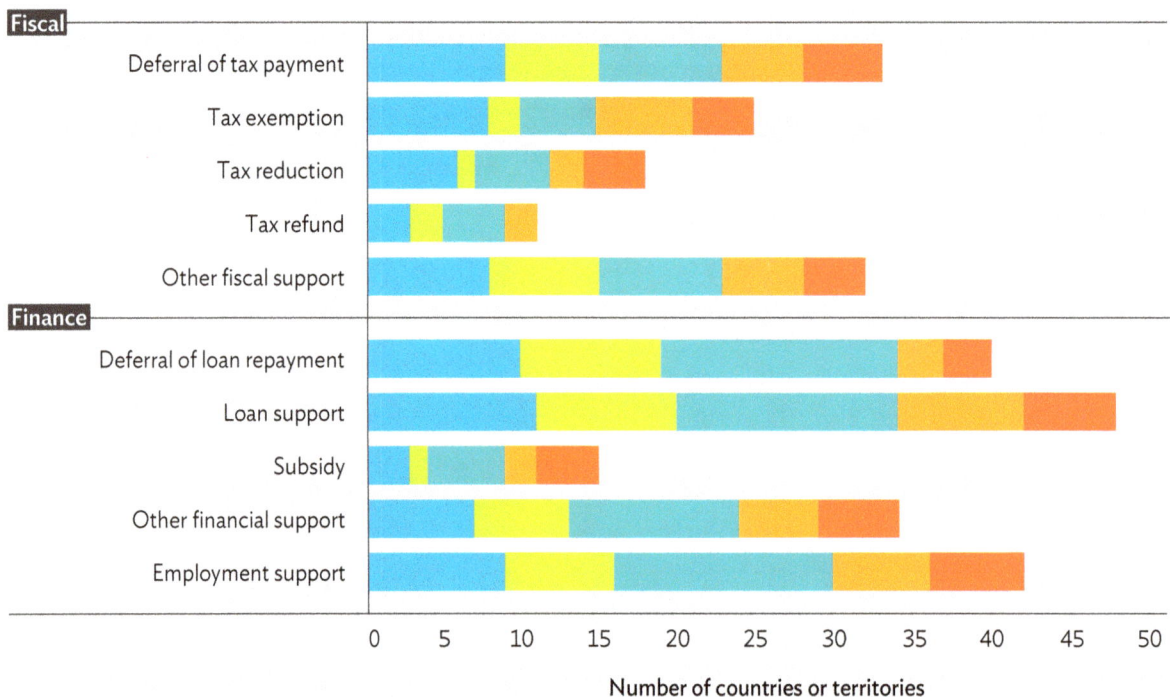

Asia and Pacific subregions

■ Southeast Asia   ■ South and Southwest Asia   ■ Pacific   ■ North and Central Asia   ■ East and Northeast Asia

Sources: Economic and Social Commission for Asia and the Pacific based on information available up to 31 May 2020 from International Monetary Fund Policy Responses to coronavirus disease (COVID-19); International Labour Organization COVID-19 Country Policy Responses; Organisation for Economic Co-operation and Development Country Policy Tracker; United Nations Educational, Scientific and Cultural Organization COVID-19 Impact on Education; Oxford COVID-19 Government Response Tracker; and various national sources and news.

Credit Guarantee Scheme Response to COVID-19 Crisis in Asia and the Pacific

As evidenced by Figure 14, loan support is the most used tool. Building upon the discussion, guarantee schemes are most agile to deploy and are one of the least market-distorting mechanisms. Economies across Asia and the Pacific have swiftly rolled out credit guarantee schemes to support SMEs. Response included prompt disbursal (pre-approved loans), concessional interest rates, loan moratoriums, waiver of guarantee fees, increased coverage in percentage and amount, and inclusion of sectors (Table 19).

Table 19: **Summary of Guarantee Measures Adopted in Selected Asia and Pacific Economies for COVID-19**

Economy	Amount ($ million)	Guarantee Measures Adopted
Azerbaijan	294	■ Entrepreneurs get state guarantee for 60% of their new bank loans and the government subsidizes half of the interest on guaranteed loans from the state budget; overall, the state support is 500 million Azerbaijan manats (about $294 million).
Cambodia	200	■ The Ministry of Economy and Finance will establish a "credit guarantee fund" of $200 million. This fund may guarantee loans through banks and financial institutions using the market policy to assuage the pressure of cash flow and working capital of businesses in all sectors.
People's Republic of China	No amount/ estimate	■ On 5 June 2020, the People's Bank of China introduced a policy allowing small and micro businesses to apply for deferring their inclusive loan repayments, maturing by end-2020 to 31 March 2021, with penalty payment exempted by providing 1% of the capital of SMEs' loan applying for deferring repayments as the incentives for the local small and medium-sized commercial banks who lent those loans. SMEs that benefit from this measure should keep effective guarantee or alternative arrangements, use the loans for production and business purposes, and promise to maintain employment stable.
Fiji	No amount/ estimate	■ The Reserve Bank of Fiji expanded the SME Credit Guarantee Scheme to assist small entities.
Georgia	109	■ 500 million lari will be provided to support businesses, including through the credit guarantee scheme. Financing for working capital will increase.
Hong Kong, China	9,066	■ Introduction of low-interest loans for small and medium-sized enterprises with 100% (HK$20 billion), 90%, and 80% guarantees from authorities. Duration to 12 months; guaranteed loans and new applications are eligible for interest subsidy for up to 12 months. ■ HK$400 million guarantee from the Anti-Epidemic Fund for the 100% Credit Limit Top-Up Scheme where the Hong Kong Export Credit Insurance Corporation increases buyers' credit limits of its policyholders by 100%.
India	40,368	■ A Credit Guarantee Scheme for PM SVANidhi was launched by the Ministry of Housing and Urban Affairs, Government of India, and administered by CGTMSE was to support urban street vendors and provide graded guarantee coverage to Member Lending Institutions to enable them to extend credit facilities to street vendors to meet their working capital requirements. G credits to Street Vendors. ■ A Credit Guarantee Scheme for Sub-Debt was launched by the Ministry of Micro, Small & Medium Enterprise, Government of India, and administered by CGTMSE to support stressed MSMEs. The objective of the scheme is to provide personal loan through banks to the promoters of stressed MSMEs for infusion as equity/quasi equity in the business eligible for restructuring. ■ 13 May 2020, ₹3 trillion worth of loan guarantees for small and medium-sized companies.
Indonesia	16,453	■ The third stimulus package includes Rp150 trillion (0.9% of GDP) additional financing for a national economic program, including to support credit guarantees for the private sector. The Indonesian Exports Financing Agency announced it will provide credit guarantees for PT Bank Mandiri Tbk to increase export financing to support the National Economic Recovery program. ■ On 7 July 2020, Rp123.46 trillion UMKM credit guarantee program for working capital loans under the National Economic Recovery Plan. Guarantees for working capital loans provided by banks for debtors, especially MSMEs.

continued on next page

Table 19: *Continued*

Economy	Amount ($ million)	Guarantee Measures Adopted
Japan	No amount/ estimate	■ For SMEs having a decline in sales of 20% or more from the previous year, they are eligible to make use of a financing guarantee up to 100% under a framework of up to 280 million yen, which is separate from a general financing guarantee. ■ Japan also included almost all sectors as eligible for its guarantee financing program.
Kazakhstan	No amount/ estimate	■ Medium-sized enterprises may apply for a loan of up to T1 billion ($2.2 million) with a state guarantee of up to 50%. ■ Micro and small enterprises may obtain loans of up to T360 million ($0.8 million) with guarantees of up to 85%.
Republic of Korea	14,000	■ A key industry stabilization fund would be established for W40 trillion (2.1% of GDP) and operated by the Korea Development Bank to support seven key industries (airlines, shipping, shipbuilding, autos, general machinery, electric power, and communications) through loans, payment guarantees, and investments. ■ W420 billion "Win–Win Guarantee Program" for SMEs through the Technology Guarantee Fund including support of up to W3 billion in working capital and up to W10 billion in facility funds. ■ Expansion of financial loans and guarantees for SMEs and affected households and businesses (W58 trillion). ■ W300 billion in guarantees by the Korea Credit Guarantee Fund (KODIT) as part of a financial aid package for the auto industry.
Malaysia	18,040	■ The government will provide a RM50 billion guarantee scheme up to 80% of the loan amount for financing working capital requirements. The minimum guaranteed loan size is RM20 million per company. ■ $7.52 million as a guarantee under the Supply Chain Finance Program (additional financing). ■ CGC Berhad Malaysia providing loan to SMEs up to RM1 million/SME, 5.5 years maximum, with 6 months moratorium on principal and interest, 80% coverage. ■ 28 June 2021 in PEMULIH, the government increased the ceiling of its guarantee scheme from RM10 billion to RM36.5 billion to assist SMEs in 2021.
Mongolia	39	■ Guarantees to support vulnerable businesses amounting to $39 million.
Philippines	2,455	■ ₱120 billion credit guarantee for affected small businesses. As of end-June 2020, P37.5 billion in guarantees have been approved. Also approved the assignment of a zero-risk weight for MSME loans guaranteed by the Philippine Guarantee Corp., Agricultural Guarantee Fund Pool, and the Agricultural Credit Policy Council.
Sri Lanka	No amount/ estimate	■ The government and the Monetary Board of the Central Bank of Sri Lanka provided construction sector enterprises with a facility to borrow from licensed commercial banks using guarantees issued by the government equivalent to the amount due on account of contracts carried out in the past, made available at the concessionary rate of 1% a year, for 180 days. ■ On 26 June 2020, the Monetary Board of the Central Bank of Sri Lanka decided to implement a Credit Guarantee and Interest Subsidy Scheme to accelerate lending by banks to businesses adversely affected by the COVID-19 pandemic. Through this scheme, the Central Bank of Sri Lanka will provide a credit guarantee to banks, ranging from 80% for smaller loans to 50% for relatively large loans to provide loans at an interest rate of 4% using the banks' own funds.
Thailand	10,901	■ The government covers the first 6 months of interest and guarantees up to 60%–70% of the B500 billion loan.
Timor-Leste	4	■ Extended access to the Credit Guarantee System to microenterprises, increasing the type of economic activities eligible for the program. The present value of the credit guarantee scheme is $4 million, but the Timorese government will inject more liquidity in the future.
Viet Nam	No amount/ estimate	■ Government guarantees for loans to aviation businesses with outstanding loans as of 31 December 2019. ■ ADB program: $415.07 million worth of loans and guarantees under the Trade Finance Program (additional financing).

₹ = Indian rupee; ₱ = Philippine peso; ADB = Asian Development Bank; B = baht; CGC = Credit Guarantee Corporation; CGTMSE = Credit Guarantee Fund Trust for Micro and Small Enterprises; COVID-19 = coronavirus disease; GDP = gross domestic product; HK$ = Hong Kong dollars; MSMEs = micro, small, and medium-sized enterprises; RM = ringgit; Rp = rupiah; SMEs = small and medium-sized enterprises; T = tenge; UMKM = micro, small, and medium enterprises (Usaha Mikro, Kecil, Menengah); W = won.

Sources: Authors (as of 3 November 2021); Asian Development Bank. COVID-19 Policy Tracker.

Credit Guarantee Scheme Response to COVID-19 Crisis Outside Asia and the Pacific

Countries worldwide have taken extensive steps to extend credit guarantees. Many countries ended up establishing credit guarantee funds to tackle the challenges posed by the COVID-19 crisis (Table 20).

Table 20: COVID-19 Responses Outside Asia and the Pacific

Country	Amount ($ million)	Guarantee Measures Adopted
Brazil	3,000	■ Guarantees loans for micro and small enterprises in the National Support Program for Micro and Small Enterprises (Pronampe). ☐ Up to 85% of guarantee, revenue cap of 30% of gross 2019 revenue cap, a 36-month term with 8-month grace period, preserve employees.
Croatia	114	■ For loans below €800,000, 10 basis points guarantee fee, with a term between 1 and 5 years and 90% guarantee on working capital loan only. ☐ For loans above €800,000, 100 basis points guarantee fee, 1- and 5-year term, maximum 90% guarantee on the loan principal if losses are shared or 35% if losses first attributed to the state.
Finland	4,513	■ Companies operating for a maximum of 3 years. ☐ Coverage ratio is up to 80% ☐ Guarantee fee of maximum 1.75%, service fee is reduced to 0.1% ☐ Minimum loan size is €10,000, the maximum guarantee is €80,000 ☐ Different conditions for a firm operating for more than 3 years
France	365,265	■ Companies of all sizes with loan size up to 3 months of 2019 turnover or 2 years of payroll for companies created after January 2019.
Germany	535,221	■ New scheme ☐ Loans up to €800,000 have 10-year terms, more than €800,000 have 6-year terms. ☐ 100% coverage ratio; 3% interest up to €800,000 ☐ Companies having more than 10 employees ☐ No repayment for the first 2 years "Limitless"
Italy	477,301	■ Increased term to 10 years from 6 years ☐ Up to €800,000 loan amount for 100% guarantee, 90% for less than 5,000 employees and €1.5 billion turnover or less; 80% for more than 5,000 employees and €1.5–5.0 billion turnover, and 70% for other firms ☐ Prohibited from dividends ☐ Guarantee fee of 25 basis points (bps) for year 1, 50 basis points for year 2–3, 100 basis points for year 4–6
Lithuania	124	■ Loan size maximum of €5 million, double the annual wage bill, 25% of annual turnover ■ For a higher coverage ratio, higher guarantee fees in all 6 years (90%) or a lower guarantee fee for an 80% coverage ratio
Peru	17,220	■ Guarantee scheme for microenterprises and working capital only ☐ Increased coverage on 27 April and expanded the number of eligible firms by allowing those with a "Normal" rating to borrow ☐ Increased the number of eligible lenders by allowing entities with a risk rating equal or higher to a C– ☐ 3 years with 1-year moratorium

continued on next page

Table 20: *Continued*

Country	Amount ($ million)	Guarantee Measures Adopted
South Africa	12,051	■ 1-year deferral, 5-year term ☐ Allows for loans with a maximum of 100 million South African rand, allows banks to provide syndicated loans larger than 50 million rand ☐ Bank credit assessments made more discretionary; business restart loans included ☐ Longer period to access the loan; interest and capital repayment holiday extended
Spain	160,642	■ New program: ☐ Part of a broader €200 billion package (of which €117 billion from state, €83 billion from the private sector) ☐ Five tranches, released over time ☐ Each tranche had different breakdowns (e.g., of the €15.5 billion of the final tranche, €7.5 billion is allocated for SMEs and the self-employed, €2.5 million for SMEs in the tourism industry, and €500 million for the automotive industry, with the remaining funding open to all firms).
Sweden	10,283	■ New program: ☐ 70% guarantee ☐ Targets SMEs though there is no size restriction ☐ Swedish National Debt Office will administer the guarantee ☐ 75 million Swedish krona maximum though exceptions can be granted
Switzerland	44,547	■ 10% of annual turnover up to CHF500,000 ☐ 0% interest ☐ Fast-track process ■ For loans between CHF500,000 and CHF20 million, 85% guarantee and bank retention of 15%. Interest rate of 0.5%.
Turkey	7,700	■ Existing program expanded: ☐ Treasury-backed credit guarantee fund to was doubled in size to 50 billion Turkish lira ($7.7 billion)
United Kingdom	1,230	■ Modified scheme so that insufficient security does not prevent access to the scheme ■ Additional accredited lenders added over time ■ £250,000 and below loans do not allow personal guarantees ■ Up to £5 million for a 6-year term ■ Government covers 12 months of interest and lender-levied charges ■ No guarantee fees to access the scheme

€ = euro, £ = pounds sterling, CHF = Swiss francs, COVID-19 = coronavirus disease, SMEs = small and medium-sized enterprises.

Sources: Authors' compilation (figures as of 31 August 2020); Yale School of Management; ADB COVID-19 Policy Tracker.

Lessons from Key Credit Guarantee Schemes around the World

Although CGS models have been operating to address SMEs' limited access to finance, some models, such as the Vietnamese CGS model, have not been very successful in facilitating wider access to SME financing. Dang and Chuc (2019) found that the most considerable challenge for the CGS in Viet Nam was the lack of concrete cooperation and risk-sharing between CGSs and involved banks. This was worsened by ineffective credit assessments that may have increased administration costs and risks. Another hurdle was the strict conditions and requirements implemented by financial institutions, which discourage SMEs to borrow.

In addition, the coverage guarantee ratio in Viet Nam is not clearly determined and regulated, which leads to difficulties in differentiating the credit risk level between banks and SMEs. The Viet Nam CGS also does not have clear conditions under which lenders can claim a guarantee, leading to disputes in the guarantee process. Additional obstacles include incompetence of staff delivering credit assessment, which makes the approval of guaranteed loans unreliable, and the current regulations of the local CGS in the Bac Ninh Province, which limits the credit guarantee activities.

Other countries, such as Japan, the Republic of Korea, and Malaysia, have shared their success stories and were able to identify effective factors that contributed to the success of CGS in their respective economies. A public–private partnership model which combined public sector presence with risk management and private sector expertise is a desirable governance structure and has greatly contributed to the success of CGS in Malaysia and the Republic of Korea. Participation of regional governments in Japan and the Republic of Korea has increased the operating efficiency of the CGS through the creation of an intra-country market.

The CGS in Japan and the Republic of Korea offered a variety of products and services to SMEs, which widened SME access to finance and enhance prudent risk management practices. Competent, experienced, and sufficient staff also helped the CGS in managing loan appraisals effectively and efficiently. In addition, the CGSs in Japan, the Republic of Korea, and Malaysia have compiled extensive databases, which eases the credit risk assessment of banks and SMEs and improves guarantee pricing mechanisms. The Industrial Bank of Korea has a legal mandate to hold 70% SME loans in its total loan portfolio, so the government provides funds and guarantees to cover deficits, enhanced schemes in the country.

Based on lessons from other economies, the advantages of the CGS include: (i) the leverage effect, (ii) regulatory capital relief, and (iii) countercyclical relief during crises. The high leverage ratio of the CGS suggests an efficient use of limited public funds. This creates a multiplier effect and reaches more benefactors.

Another advantage is that most CGSs are backed by government guarantees, making them eligible to receive a 0% risk weight for the loan's guaranteed portion. This significantly reduces the regulatory capital cost to lenders.

In addition, during the 1997 Asian financial crisis, the 2008 global financial crisis (GFC), and the COVID-19 pandemic crisis, CGS is often first to respond and plays a key countercyclical role by supporting SMEs despite uncertainty among lenders.

However, while the CGS is among the most successful and feasible market-friendly interventions, as these countries illustrate, it should not be set up as a quick-cure for underlying market failure. Rather, the scheme should be set up and operated within the existing financial environment and tailor-fit to the country.

The recent pandemic has pushed economies to take certain safeguards to ensure that CGS loans would achieve their intended purpose and prevent misuse. Croatia advises guarantee coverage up to 90% if the state bears the first loss. In Finland, there are different conditions for firms operating under and above 3 years. A higher guarantee fee for 6 years for 90% coverage or lower guarantee for 80% coverage.

The case studies analyzed and presented in the publication look at CGSs in 6 countries in Asia as well as the US and the EU. These give several insights into different legal and regulatory framework, corporate governance, services and products offered, and the credit risk management practices.

- First, differences in organizational models are stark and reflect varying political and financial systems. Countries had the option to form public-private partnerships or private mutual guarantee schemes.

- Second, the choice of risk assessment and organizational model had an impact on the strength and professionalism of staff in the CGS.

- Third, the CGS gave advisory services to SMEs, which aided long-term performance and made finance more accessible.

- Fourth, better managed CGSs committed to a leverage ratio and transparency about their risk and operations. Successes in Japan, the Republic of Korea, and Malaysia have proven that good risk assessment capabilities anchored on information from extensive databases on borrower risk contributed to sustainable guaranteed income.

- The EU case shows that the private mutual guarantee schemes formed by SMEs reduced information asymmetry with lending institutions.

As learned, adequate financial strength and prudent risk management practices in a CGS is important to widen financial access to SMEs. Specifically, in the Vietnamese case, coordination and risk-sharing between public and private stakeholders in assessing credit and managing loans must be strengthened.

Case studies also suggest that credit assessment should be facilitated by private entities for the CGS to arrive at rational decisions about SME eligibility for a guaranteed loan. The CGS should also employ proper coverage ratios to encourage the lender to carefully screen and monitor the loans covered by the guarantee scheme. This will help prevent moral hazard to both financial institutions and SMEs.

In addition, CGS staff assessing SME credit must have sufficient capacity, experience in customer management, and appraisal and analysis skills for accurate and objective assessment of loan guarantees.

Most importantly, the CGS must never forget its mandate and reconstruct the credit guarantee conditions to allow more bank loans to SMEs. This should be accompanied by a credit information center that is useful for guarantors to evaluate whether the SME is financially sound and healthy to prevent delay in loan repayment, leading to higher levels of NPLs.

Outlook

While the use of the CGS is required at this juncture, policy makers should be cautious. On a primary analysis done on the current amount of guaranteed loans compared to existing debt levels, many economies, especially high-income, have already amassed substantial guarantees (Figure 15). This gains more prominence as guaranteed loans are only one package adopted by governments to deal with the COVID-19 crisis.

On a note of caution, guaranteed programs can alleviate short-term liquidity problems, but their effectiveness and sustainability ultimately depend on improving macroeconomic conditions.

Figure 15: COVID-19 Response: Guaranteed Loan versus Debt Level

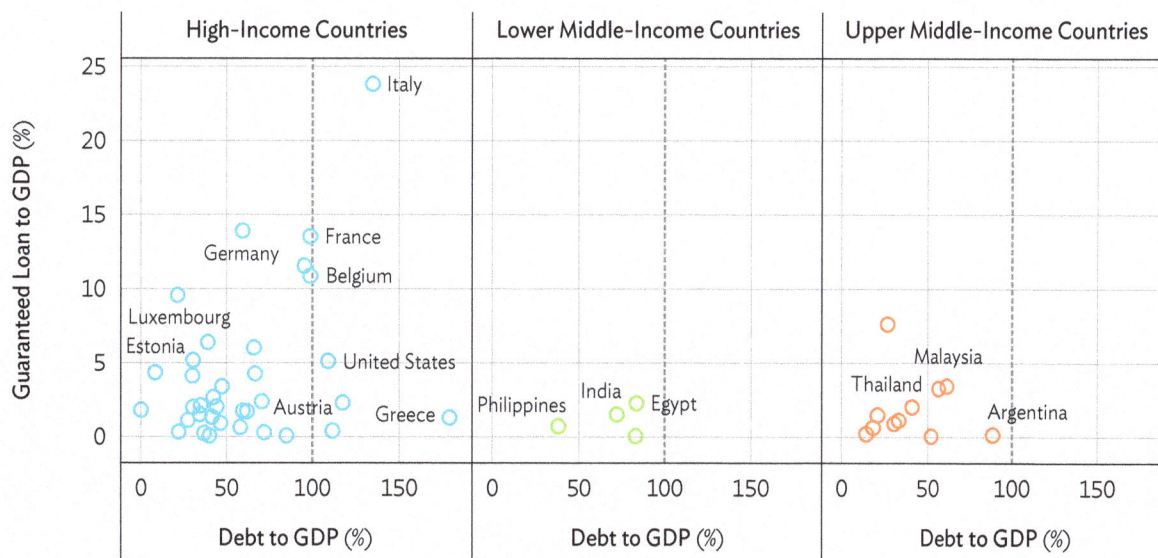

COVID-19 = coronavirus disease, GDP = gross domestic product.
Source: Authors' compilation. Data from World Bank. https://data.worldbank.org/; IMF. https://www.imf.org/; and the Asian Development Bank. https://www.adb.org/.

XV CONCLUSION AND RECOMMENDATIONS

SMEs, as we have covered extensively in this publication, are a critical and inseparable part of the enterprise ecosystem. They provide large-scale employment, contribute to GDP, and help nations compete through exports in this globalized world. In an economic growth engine, finance functions like oil in a mechanical machine. Yet, enterprises and SMEs face hurdles in accessing this critical financing.

This publication has extensively discussed the multiple factors impacting SME access to finance: the internal (governance, accounting, financial expertise, etc.) and external (credit support regulatory norms, lack of diversified financial institutions, etc.).

The Asian credit ecosystem is still very heavily bank-dominated in most developing countries in Asia and the Pacific, and nonbank financial institutions have a very limited presence. Further, institutions such as venture capital funds or well-developed capital markets have a very limited presence in most, with noted and promising exceptions in countries such as Japan and the Republic of Korea.

Further, support is limited in this region for credit infrastructure such as credit and collateral registries that could ease the severe information asymmetry issues that are frequently behind poor credit access.

The only supporting institutional credit mechanism that has a relatively wider presence in Asia's developing countries are CGSs. The CGS has commendably bridged information asymmetry and widened SME access to credit. The schemes work basically by sharing the default risk of borrowers with financial institutions, which helps SMEs overcome the hurdles of conventional credit assessment standards and institutional preferences that arose out of "legacy" processes.

CGSs have evolved and, in addition to sharing default-risk as a product, have leveraged their central positioning in financial ecosystems to provide other products and services that improve financial access to SMEs. These include products such as trade insurance, direct lending, and consultancy services on financial and/or management issues to SMEs. These services allow smaller firms to better project and leverage their core strengths and expertise and obtain better access for both markets and credit.

Some CGSs have also evolved to serve as credit information bureaus and credit registries, which helps SMEs obtain reliable estimates of their "actual" riskiness and credit from financial institutions. Notable success stories include Japan's Credit Risk Database and Malaysia's Credit Bureau, among others.

The publication looked at six countries in Asia: the People's Republic of China, India, Japan, the Republic of Korea, Malaysia, and Sri Lanka. It also looked at the European Union and the United States. It scrutinized organizational structures, staff strength and expertise, funding models, risk management practices, and the extent of services offered by the CGS.

The public component in CGSs is one of the most common factors and a public–private partnership model that complements public sector presence with risk management and private sector expertise is a desirable governance structure (the Republic of Korea, Malaysia).

Also prominent in advanced CGSs, such as in Japan and the Republic of Korea, is the participation of provincial governments. As CGSs mature, the increased involvement of regional governments not only lends the desired diversification of funding and governance, but also increases CGS operating efficiency by creating an intra-country market.

The European Union presents an alternative model of the government taking a supporting role in multiple regions, with private mutual guarantee societies flourishing in the region.

Older and relatively successful CGSs, such as in Japan, the Republic of Korea, and Malaysia, also offer a menu of services for SMEs, which help these firms access finance and helped the schemes run efficiently with prudent risk management practices.

Full-fledged and healthy staff presence also helped in the performance of these CGS. Successful countries also paid considerable attention to pricing and risk management practices, which helped in the long-run sustainability of schemes. However, some countries had comparatively less success with the CGS, as market participants shied away from the schemes due to claims-management issues.

The publication also discusses the impact of the CGS in a rigorous setup, examining ample studies from across the globe that established the financial and economic additionality of CGSs. The CGS, if executed well and in sync with prudent principles of risk management and governance, delivers a multi-faceted and positive impact on employment, terms of credit, GDP growth, tax revenues, and many other factors. These success stories were observed both for developed and developing nations, which makes the CGS a potent tool for policy makers.

Policy recommendations to set up and operate CGSs rest on two cornerstones: (i) a "unique and important" exercise to "soul-search" the purpose and positioning of the CGS; and (ii) "prudent principles" to be followed while setting up and running the schemes.

First, the "soul-searching" step is a crucial first step and seeks to identify the priority areas to target only those where it can function most efficiently. This process is concerned with establishing a CGS within the context of each country's unique financial, legal, and regulatory environment. This should complement existing institutions of the country and its socio-political setup, government preference, and capacity constraints. These factors determine the CGS's objectives and affect its ownership structure (i.e., public or private) and governance, and the range of services it should offer.

For example, countries with a weak public sector should consider engaging with the private sector and international organizations, while countries with low financial and business literacy can provide advisory services alongside loan guarantees to improve financial reporting standards and increase lender confidence. This exercise is important to reveal optimum and key areas in which the CGS can have a positive impact.

After recognizing this "soul", the CGS must run on a series of "prudent principles" to ensure it does not drag on the finances of the country, leaving SMEs in the same or a worse position. There are three: (i) legal and regulatory setup and corporate governance; (ii) services offered; and (iii) risk management, and monitoring and evaluation.

A strong legal and corporate governance foundation and range of services offered should be established in the short-term horizon alongside the "soul-searching" stage. First, legal and corporate governance aim to create an enabling environment for CGS operations and SME access to credit. The organizational setup of the CGS must be robustly and unambiguously backed up by a legal act that establishes a clear regulatory and supervisory system, while the board and governance should appropriately reflect the risks undertaken and policies the same.

Second, services offered should appropriately reflect the findings of the "soul-searching" exercise. One of the most important factors in determining the scope of services is establishing a list of firms and SMEs eligible for guarantee support. The establishment of sufficient eligibility criteria should be both a short-term and long-term target horizon. In the short term the CGS may begin by targeting firms that have easier availability of data. In the long-term they can leverage this data so that they may build their risk pricing and management system and grow with time—such is the case of CGC Berhad Malaysia and Credit Bureau Malaysia.

The last salient feature, concerned with risk management, and monitoring and evaluation, is also both a short-term and long-term concern, where a risk management and monitoring framework should be established at the onset of a CGS, but its key performance indicators should be looked at with a longer-term perspective. A CGS should not be too rigid in meeting the short-term risk management framework at the expense of achieving its main objective of increasing SME access to finance. Cases of CGS support around the globe show the importance of flexible eligibility criteria in supporting emergency liquidity scenarios.

In that vein, a CGS should be focused on generating a high fee income and high leverage ratio. This guarantees high utilization of funds and correct risk pricing on SME exposures. A study of income sources to examine financial sustainability make clear that the most desired state for the CGS is having a high share of guarantee fee income and high leverage ratios. This contributes immensely to sustainability (Kim et al. 2021).

At the same time, a CGS must have a robust monitoring and evaluation framework for a strong feedback loop and to justify public support that it might be getting in its operations. The strength of a monitoring and evaluation framework will be crucial in the post-pandemic scenario when CGS across the globe will face rising default rates in conjunction with the lifting of debt moratoriums and forbearance measures and slowing of accommodative monetary and fiscal policies.

COVID-19 has harshly impacted both the financial and real sectors, although the exact magnitude remains to be ascertained. SMEs are among the hardest hit as they have fewer financing options, less diversified businesses, more dependence on credit, precarious working capital cycles, and other issues. As discussed earlier, due to the critical economic role of SMEs in the economy, governments have moved swiftly to help SMEs hold on and survive.

In this, with such a strong and central role in financial ecosystems, it is no wonder that the CGS is a preferred and one of the most extensive tools used by government. These schemes are uniquely and centrally placed in financial ecosystems, having functional business relationships with both SMEs and financial institutions. These relationships can be leveraged to navigate uncertainty that would normally paralyze business decisions. In addition, CGS support usually requires no or less-immediate cash flows, which allows governments to support SMEs without incurring significant fiscal costs in the present. Further, the range of CGS policy tools can be tailored for SMEs and banks, depending upon the needs of the businesses and the country.

The publication has noted that during major past crises—global financial crisis and Asian financial crisis—countries used the CGS extensively to support SMEs. Italy, Japan, the Republic of Korea, and others extended guarantees in terms of amounts and coverage ratios. Finland, Hungary, and other EU countries suspended guarantee fees, as did the US Small Business Administration.

It is thus no surprise that in the COVID-19 crisis, CGSs have been well favored as a policy tool in Asia and around the world. Response to COVID-19 fits into two broad buckets: to address issues of "systemic loss aversion" and "issues with SME businesses." The former entails increasing coverage ratio (Hong Kong, China; Kazakhstan; Malaysia; the Philippines; and others), expanding to new firms and sectors (France, Japan, the Republic of Korea, and others), change in risk-weights (the Philippines), launching new schemes and funds (Cambodia, Sri Lanka), and relaxed assessment standards (Peru, the UK).

Measures addressing the latter—issues with SME businesses—entail increasing loan tenors and extending moratoriums (Australia, India, Thailand, and others). They include increasing maximum coverage amounts (Georgia, Japan, the Republic of Korea, and others), removing or reducing guarantee fees (India, the Philippines, the UK, and others), concessional interest rates (Azerbaijan, Latvia, Thailand, and others), and reducing collateral requirements (Bulgaria, the UK).

Developing countries in Asia and the Pacific, in particular, have used the CGS as a policy tool extensively, and increasing coverage ratios and loan tenors and moratoriums have been the most preferred response. This is followed by concessional lending rates and expanding to new categories and sectors.

To balance speed and accuracy during crisis, certain relaxations are extended in identifying and extending benefits. As behavioral finance and experience during past crises tells us, however, market participants are not above moral hazard or exploiting information asymmetry. As such, countries have taken safeguard measures to contain such issues arising during COVID-19 CGS operations.

To address moral hazard, Italy prohibits firms availing the benefits from distributing dividends. Similarly, in relaxed due diligence standards or reckless lending, Belgium advises that first losses up to a certain percentage will be borne by lenders, even though the government will bear the substantial portion of overall losses. To address information asymmetry in firms, Japan made SMEs eligible in which sales declined 20% or more from the previous year.

It is fitting to close by reiterating an established public policy principle: "every crisis is an opportunity for reform." Countries, while dealing with COVID-19, must recognize the immense advantages of the CGS in helping SMEs, one of the most critical components of an economy. Since developing countries usually lack the fiscal space of advanced economies, Asia's developing economies need to pay more attention to CGSs to maximize scarce fiscal resources and transition SMEs out of this pandemic and back onto a growth path.

APPENDIX

Table A.1: Micro, Small, and Medium-Sized Enterprise Definitions in Selected Asia and Pacific Countries
(number of employees)

Country	Class	Micro	Small	Medium	Large
Bangladesh	LMIC	<10 services; <25 manufacturing	10–24 services; 25–99 manufacturing	50–100 services; 100–250 manufacturing	>100 services; >250 manufacturing
Cambodia	LMIC	1–10	11–50	51–100	>100
People's Republic of China	UMIC	<5 wholesale; <10 retail, accommodation, restaurant, information, software, tenancy, other; <20 heavy industry, transportation, warehouse, postal; <100 property management	5–20 wholesale; 10–50 retail; 20–100 warehouse; 10–100 accommodation, restaurant, software, tenancy, information, other; 20–300 heavy industry, transportation, postal; 100–300 property management	20–200 wholesale; 50–300 retail; 100–200 warehouse; 100–300 accommodation, restaurant, software, tenancy, other; 100–2,000 information; 300–1,000 heavy industry, transportation, postal, property management	>200 wholesale; >200 warehouse; >300 accommodation, restaurant, software, tenancy, retail, other; >1,000 heavy industry, transportation, postal, property management; >2,000 information
Fiji	UMIC	0–6	7–20	21–50	>50
India	LMIC	1–10	10–50	50–250	>250
Indonesia	UMIC	1–4	5–19	20–99	>99
Kazakhstan	UMIC	<100	<100	101–250	>250
Republic of Korea	HIC	<10 in manufacturing, mining, construction, transportation; <5 in other	<50 in manufacturing, mining, construction, transportation; <10 in other	<300 manufacturing, mining, construction, transportation; <200 agriculture; <100 others; <50 real estate	≥300 manufacturing, mining, construction, transportation; ≥200 agriculture; ≥100 others; ≥50 real estate
Kyrgyz Republic	LMIC	Microenterprises include individual entrepreneurs and farms.	<50 in agriculture, hunting and forestry; fishing and fish farming; mining industry; manufacturing industry; production and distribution of electricity, gas, and water; construction. <15 at enterprises engaged in trade; repair of cars, household goods and personal items; the provision of services by hotels and restaurants; on transport and communications; financial activities; real estate transactions, rental and provision of services to consumers; education; health care and the provision of social services; by providing communal, social and personal services.	51–200 in agriculture, hunting and forestry; fishing and fish farming; mining industry; manufacturing industry; production and distribution of electricity, gas, and water; construction. 16–50 at enterprises engaged in trade; repair of cars, household goods and personal items; the provision of services by hotels and restaurants; on transport and communications; financial activities; real estate transactions, rental and provision of services to consumers; education; health care and the provision of social services; by providing communal, social and personal services.	–

continued on next page

Table A.1: *Continued*

Country	Class	Micro	Small	Medium	Large
Lao People's Democratic Republic	LMIC	–	≤19	20–99	>99
Malaysia	UMIC	<5	5–75 manufacturing; 5–30 services and others	76–200 manufacturing; 31–75 services and others	>200 manufacturing; >76 services and others
Mongolia	LMIC	≤19 trade/service	≤19 manufacturing; ≤49 service	≤149 wholesale trade; ≤199 retail trade, manufacturing	>149 wholesale trade; >199 retail trade, manufacturing
Papua New Guinea	LMIC	–	–	<500	>500
Philippines	LMIC	1–9	10–99	100–199	>199
Solomon Islands	LMIC	1–19	20–49	>49	–
Sri Lanka	LMIC	1–4 industry, construction, services; 1–3 trade	5–24 industry, construction; 5–15 services; 4–14 trade	25–199 industry, construction; 15–34 trade; 16–74 services	>199 industry, construction; >34 trade; >74 services
Tajikistan	LIC	<1	1–30	30–200	>200
Thailand	UMIC	–	≤50 manufacturing, services; ≤25 wholesale; ≤15 retail	51–200 manufacturing, services; 26–50 wholesale; 16–30 retail	>200 manufacturing, services; >50 wholesale; >30 retail
Viet Nam	LMIC	<11	10–200 agriculture, industry, construction; 10–50 commerce, services	201–300 agriculture, industry, construction; 50–100 commerce, services	>300 agriculture, industry, construction; >100 commerce, services

– = data not available, HIC = high-income country, LIC = low-income country, LMIC = lower middle-income country, UMIC = upper middle-income country.

Source: SME Finance Forum. MSME Economic Indicators. https://www.smefinanceforum.org/ (accessed 22 November 2021).

Table A.2: Micro, Small, and Medium-Sized Enterprise Definitions in Selected Asian Countries
(assets, local currency, unless otherwise noted)

Country	Class	Micro	Small	Medium	Large	Currency
Bangladesh	LMIC	<500,000 services; <5,000,000 manufacturing	500,000–10,000,000 services; 5,000,000–100,000,000 manufacturing	10,000,000–150,000,000 services; 100,000,000–300,000,000 manufacturing	>150,000,000 services; >300,000,000 manufacturing	taka (Tk)
People's Republic of China	UMIC	<3,000,000 construction; <20,000,000 real estate; <1,000,000 leasing and commercial services	3,000,000–50,000,000 construction; 20,000,000–50,000,000 real estate; 1,000,000–80,000,000 leasing and commercial services	50,000,000–800,000,000 construction; 50,000,000–100,000,000 real estate; 80,000,000–120,000,000 leasing and commercial services	>800,000,000 construction; >100,000,000 real estate; >120,000,000 leasing and commercial services	yuan (CNY)
India	LMIC	Investment in Plant and Machinery or Equipment: Not more than ₹1 crore and Annual Turnover; not more than ₹5 crore	Investment in Plant and Machinery or Equipment: Not more than ₹10 crore and Annual Turnover; not more than ₹50 crore	Investment in Plant and Machinery or Equipment: Not more than ₹50 crore and Annual Turnover; not more than ₹250 crore	Investment in Plant and Machinery or Equipment: Above ₹50 crore and Annual Turnover; Above ₹250 crore	Indian rupee (₹)
Indonesia	UMIC	<50,000,000	50,000,000–500,000,000	500,000,001–10,000,000,000	>10,000,000,000	rupiah (Rp)
Republic of Korea	HIC	<8,000,000,000 manufacturing; <3,000,000,000 mining, construction, transportation	–	–	≥8,000,000,000 manufacturing; ≥3,000,000,000 mining, construction, transportation	won (W)
Lao People's Democratic Republic	LMIC	–	≤250,000,000	250,000,001–1,200,000,000	>1,200,000,000	kip (KN)
Philippines	LMIC	<3,000,000	3,000,000–15,000,000	15,000,001–100,000,000	>100,000,000	peso (₱)
Thailand	UMIC	–	≤50,000,000 manufacturing, services, wholesale; ≤30,000,000 retail	50,000,001–200,000,000 manufacturing, services; 50,000,001–100,000,000 wholesale; 30,000,001–60,000,000 retail	>200,000,000 manufacturing, services; >100,000,000 wholesale; >60,000,000 retail	baht (B)
Viet Nam	LMIC	–	<10,000,000,000 commerce, services; <20,000,000,000 agriculture, industry, construction	10,000,000,000–50,000,000,000 commerce, services; 20,000,000,000–100,000,000,000 agriculture, industry, construction	>50,000,000,000 commerce, services; >100,000,000,000 agriculture, industry, construction	dong (D)

HIC = high-income country, LIC = low-income country, LMIC = lower middle-income country, UMIC = upper middle-income country.

Source: SME Finance Forum. MSME Economic Indicators. https://www.smefinanceforum.org/ (accessed 22 November 2021).

Table A.3: **Micro, Small, and Medium-Sized Enterprise Definitions in Selected Asia and Pacific Countries**
(revenues)

Country	Class	Micro	Small	Medium	Large	Currency
People's Republic of China	UMIC	<500,000 software; <1,000,000 retail, warehouse, postal, accommodation, restaurant, information, real estate, tenancy; <2,000,000 transportation; <3,000,000 heavy industry, construction; <5,000,000 property management; <10,000,000 wholesale	500,000–10,000,000 software; 1,000,000–5,000,000 retail; 1,000,000–10,000,000 warehouse, information, real estate; 1,000,000–20,000,000 postal, accommodation, restaurant; 1,000,000–80,000,000 tenancy; 2,000,000–30,000,000 transportation; 3,000,000–20,000,000 heavy industry; 3,000,000–60,000,000 construction; 5,000,000–10,000,000 property management; 10,000,000–50,000,000 wholesale	10,000,0000–100,000,000 software; 5,000,000–200,000,000 retail; 10,000,000–300,000,000 warehouse; 10,000,000–1,000,000,000 information; 10,000,000–2,000,000,000 real estate; 20,000,000–300,000,000 postal; 20,000,000–100,000,000 accommodation, restaurant; 80,000,000–1,200,000,000 tenancy; 30,000,000–300,000,000 transportation; 20,000,000–400,000,000 heavy industry; 60,000,000–800,000,000 construction; 10,000,000–50,000,000 property management; 50,000,000–400,000,000 wholesale	>50,000,000 property management; >100,000,000 software, accommodation, restaurant; >200,000,000 retail; >300,000,000 warehouse, postal, transportation; >400,000,000 heavy industry, wholesale; >800,000,000 construction; >1,000,000,000 information; >1,200,000,000 tenancy; >2,000,000,000 real estate	yuan (CNY)
Fiji	UMIC	<30,000	30,000–100,000	100,000–500,000	>500,000	dollar ($)
Indonesia	UMIC	<300,000,000	300,000,000–2,500,000,000	2,500,000,001–50,000,000,000	>50,000,000,000	rupiah (Rp)
Republic of Korea	HIC	–	–	<30,000,000,000 publication, information and communication, and others; <20,000,000,000 agriculture and others; <10,000,000,000 sewerage, waste management, and others; <5,000,000,000 real estate	≥30,000,000,000 publication, information, communication, and others; ≥20,000,000,000 agriculture and others; ≥10,000,000,000 sewerage, waste management, and others; ≥5,000,000,000 real estate	won (W)
Lao People's Democratic Republic	LMIC	–	≤400,000,000	400,000,001–1,000,000,000	>1,000,000,000	kip (KN)
Malaysia	UMIC	<300,000	300,000–15,000,000 manufacturing; 300,000–3,000,000 services and others	15,000,001–50,000,000 manufacturing; 3,000,001–20,000,000 services and others	>50,000,000 manufacturing; >20,000,000 services and others	ringgit (RM)
Mongolia	LMIC	≤250,000,000 trade/service	≤250,000,000 manufacturing; ≤1,000,000 service	≤1,500,000,000 wholesale trade, retail trade, manufacturing	>1,500,000,000 wholesale trade, retail trade, manufacturing	togrog (MNT)

– = data not available, HIC = high-income country, LIC = low-income country, LMIC = lower middle-income country, UMIC = upper middle-income country.

Source: SME Finance Forum. MSME Economic Indicators. https://www.smefinanceforum.org/ (accessed 22 November 2021).

REFERENCES

Afi and CERGAS. 2010. *Analisis de la Capitalisacion del Sistema de Garantia Reciproca.* Madrid: Analista Financieros Internacionales.

Akcigit, U., U. Seven, I. Yarba, and F. Yilmaz. 2021. Firm-Level Impact of Credit Guarantees: Evidence from Turkish Credit Guarantee Fund. *Working Papers.* No. 2110. Research and Monetary Policy Department, Central Bank of the Republic of Turkey.

Allinson, G. F., P. Robson, and I. Stone. 2013. *Economic Evaluation of the Enterprise Finance Guarantee (EFG) Scheme.* Department for Business, Innovation and Skills Project Report.

Amornkitvikai, Y. and C. Harvie. 2016. *The Impact of Finance on the Performance of Thai Manufacturing Small and Medium-Sized Enterprises.* https://www.adb.org/sites/default/files/publication/185285/adbi-wp576.pdf.

Armstrong, C. E., B. R. Craig, W. E. Jackson, and J. B. Thomson. 2010. The importance of financial market development on the relationship between loan guarantees for SMEs and local market employment rates. *Federal Reserve Bank of Cleveland Working Papers (Old Series).* No. 1020. Ohio.

Artinger, F. M., S. Artinger, and G. Gigerenzer. 2018. C. Y. A.: frequency and causes of defensive decisions in public administration. *Business Research.* 12(1). pp. 9–25. https://link.springer.com/article/10.1007/s40685-018-0074-2.

Asian Development Bank (ADB). forthcoming. COVID-19 and the Finance Sector in Asia and the Pacific: Guidance Note.

———. n.d. *Viet Nam: Second Small and Medium-Sized Enterprises Development Program.* Manila. https://www.adb.org/projects/44057-013/main.

———. n.d. *Armenia: Women's Entrepreneurship Support Sector Development Program.* Manila. https://www.adb.org/projects/45230-001/main#project-overview.

———. 2014. *ADB–OECD Study on Enhancing Financial Accessibility for SMEs: Lessons from Recent Crises.* Manila.

———. 2015. *Asia Finance Monitor 2014.* Manila.

———. 2016a. *Completion Report: Second Small and Medium-Sized Enterprises Development Program in Viet Nam.* Manila.

———. 2016b. *Credit guarantees: Challenging their role in improving access to finance in the Pacific region.* Manila.

———. 2017. *Technical Assistance Consultant's Report to Sri Lanka for Small and Medium-Sized Enterprises Line of Credit Project.* Manila.

———. 2018. *Completion Report: Women's Entrepreneurship Support Sector Development Program in Armenia.* Manila.

———. 2019. Credit Guarantee System Expands Finance for Mongolia's SMEs. Video. Manila. https://www.adb.org/news/videos/credit-guarantee-system-expands-finance-mongolia-s-smes.

———. 2020a. *Asia Small and Medium-Sized Enterprise Monitor 2020: Volume I—Country and Regional Reviews.* Manila.

———. 2020b. *Validation Report: Second Investment Climate Improvement Program (Subprograms 1–3) in Kyrgyz Republic.* Independent Evaluation Department. Manila: ADB.

Banerjee, A., S. Cole, and E. Duflo. 2007. *Are the monitors over-monitored: Evidence from Corruption, Vigilance, and Lending in Indian Banks.* https://www.researchgate.net/publication/228717204_Are_the_monitors_over-monitored_Evidence_from_Corruption_Vigilance_and_Lending_in_Indian_Banks.

Bank for International Settlements. 2006. *Basel II: International Convergence of Capital Measurement and Capital Standards: A Revised Framework.* Basel. https://www.bis.org/publ/bcbs128.htm.

Bank of Japan (BOJ). 2020. *Tankan Statistics.* https://www.boj.or.jp/en/statistics/tk/index.htm/ (accessed 2020).

Beck, T., L. F. Klapper, and J. C. Mendoza. 2008. The Typology of Partial Credit Guarantee Funds around the World. *World Bank Policy Research Working Paper.* No. 4771. Washington, DC.

———. 2010. The Typology of Partial Credit Guarantee Funds around the World. *Journal of Financial Stability Elsevier.* 6(1). pp. 10–25.

Benavente, J., A. Galetovic, and R. Sanhueza. 2006. *FOGAPE: An Economic Analysis.*

Berger, A. N. and G. F. Udell. 2004. The institutional memory hypothesis and the procyclicality of bank lending behavior. *Journal of Financial Intermediation.* 13(4). pp. 458–495.

———. 2005. A More Complete Conceptual Framework for Financing of Small and Medium Enterprises. *The World Bank Policy Research Working Paper Series.* No. 3795.

Bertoni, F., J. Brault, M. G. Colombo, A. Quas, and S. Signore. 2019. Econometric study on the impact of EU loan guarantee financial instruments on growth and jobs of SMEs. *European Investment Fund Working Paper.* No. 2019/54.

Boocock, G. and M. Shariff. 2005. Measuring the Effectiveness of Credit Guarantee Schemes. *International Small Business Journal.* 23(4). pp. 427–454.

Bradshaw, T. K. 2002. The Contribution of Small Business Loan Guarantees to Economic Development. *Economic Development Quarterly.* 16(4). pp. 360–369.

Brash, R. and M. Gallagher. 2008. *A Performance Analysis of SBA's Loan and Investment Programs.* Washington, DC: Urban Institute.

Brown, J. D. and J. S. Earle. 2017. Finance and growth at the firm level: Evidence from SBA loans. *The Journal of Finance.* 72(3). pp. 1039–1080.

Busetta, G. and A. Presbiterio. 2008. *Confidi, piccole imprese e banche: un'analisi empirica.* Rome: I vincoli finanziari alle crescita delle imprese.

Calice, P. 2016. Assessing Implementation of the Principles for Public Credit Guarantees for SMEs: A Global Survey. *World Bank Policy Research Paper*. 7753.

Caselli, S., G. Corbetta, M. Rossolini, and V. Vecchi. 2019. Public credit guarantee schemes and SMEs' profitability: Evidence from Italy. *Journal of Small Business Management*. 57(S2). pp. 555–578.

Chatzouz, M., A. Gereben, F. Lanf, and W. Torfs. 2017. Credit Guarantee Schemes for SME lending in Western Europe. *EIF Working Paper*. No. 2017/42.

Chemmanur, T. and A. Yan. 2000. Equilibrium leasing contracts under double-sided asymmetric information. *Working Paper*. Boston College.

Cowan, K., A. Drexler, and A. Yañez. 2015. The Effect of Credit Guarantees on Credit Availability and Delinquency Rates. *Journal of Banking & Finance*. 59(C). pp. 98–110.

Cowling, M. 2010. The Role of Loan Guarantee Schemes in Alleviating Credit Rationing in the UK. *Journal of Financial Stability*. 6. pp. 36–44. 10.1016/j.jfs.2009.05.007.

Craig, B. R., W. E. Jackson III, and J. B. Thompson. 2007. On Government Intervention in the Small-firm Credit Market and Its Effect on Economic Performance. *Federal Reserve Bank of Cleveland Working Paper*. No. 07–02. Ohio.

Damu. 2017. *Report on the State of Development of Small and Medium Entrepreneurship in Kazakhstan and its Regions*. Almaty.

Dang, L. and A. Chuc. 2019. Challenges in Implementing the Credit Guarantee Scheme for Small and Medium-Sized Enterprises: The Case of Viet Nam. *ADBI Working Paper*. No. 941. Tokyo.

De Alwis, S. and B. M. R. Basnayake. 2009. Credit Guarantee Schemes in Sri Lanka – Way Forward. *Journal for SME Development*. 14. pp. 51–82.

De Blasio, G., S. De Mitri, A. D'Ignazio, P. F. Russo, and L. Stoppani. 2017. Public guarantees on loans to SMEs: an RDD evaluation. *Temi di discussione (Economic working papers)*. 1111. Bank of Italy, Economic Research and International Relations Area.

Deelen, L. and K. Molenaar. 2004. *Guarantee funds for small enterprises. A manual for guarantee fund managers*. International Labour Organization.

D'Ignazio, A. and C. Menon. 2013. The causal effect of credit guarantees for SMEs: evidence from Italy. *Temi di discussione (Economic working papers)*. No. 900. Bank of Italy.

European Association of Guarantee Institutions (AECM). 2010. *Guarantees and the recovery: The impact of anti-crisis guarantee measures*. European Association of Mutual Guarantee Societies.

————. 2012. *AECM: Pricing Survey: How AECM Members Price their Guarantees?* https://aecm.eu/wp-content/uploads/2015/07/Pricing-Survey-final-results1.pdf.

European Bank for Reconstruction and Development (EBRD). 2020. *State credit guarantee schemes: Supporting SME access to finance amid the Covid-19 crisis*. London.

European Central Bank (ECB). 2018. Survey on the Access to Finance of Enterprises in the euro area – April to September 2018. https://www.ecb.europa.eu/stats/ecb_surveys/safe/html/ecb.safe201811.en.html#t.

Export–Import Bank (EXIM) Thailand. 2019. *Annual Report.* https://www.exim.go.th/getattachment/Annual-Reports/Annual_Report_2019/EXIM-AR-2562_EN.pdf.aspx.

FCI. 2020. *FCI Annual Review 2020.* https://www.smefinanceforum.org/sites/default/files/FCI%20Annual%20Review%202020%20LR.pdf.

Fellner, G., W. Güth, and B. Maciejovsky. 2009. Satisficing in financial decision making—a theoretical and experimental approach to bounded rationality. *Journal of Mathematical Psychology.* 53(1). pp. 26–33. https://www.sciencedirect.com/science/article/abs/pii/S0022249608001119.

Fisera, B., R. Horvath, and M. Melecky. 2019. Basel III Implementation and SME Financing : Evidence for Emerging Markets and Developing Economies. *The World Bank Policy Research Working Paper Series.* 9069. The World Bank.

Gottschalk, R. 2007. *Basel II implementation in developing countries – effects on SME development.* https://icrier.org/pdf/Gottschalk_presentation.pdf.

Green, A. 2003. *Credit Guarantee Schemes for Small Enterprises: An Effective Instrument to Promote Private Sector-Led Growth?* United Nations Industrial Development Organization.

Hancock, D., J. Peek, and J. A. Wilcox. 2007. The Repercussions on Small Banks and Small Businesses of Bank Capital and Loan Guarantees. *Wharton Financial Institutions Center Working Paper.* No. 07-22.

Harvie, C., D. Narjoko, and S. Oum. 2013. Small and Medium Enterprises' Access to Finance: Evidence from Selected Asian Economies. *ERIA Discussion Paper Series.* No. 2013-23. Jakarta: Economic Research Institute for ASEAN and East Asia.

Hennecke, P., D. Neuberger, and D. Ulbricht. 2017. The economic and fiscal value of German guarantee banks. *Thuenen-Series of Applied Economic Theory.* No. 152. University of Rostock.

Honohan. P. 2010. Partial credit guarantees: Principles and practice. *Journal of Financial Stability.* 6(1). pp. 1–9. https://www.sciencedirect.com/science/article/pii/S1572308909000412.

Hosono, K., K. Sakai, and K. Tsuru. 2006. Consolidation of Cooperative Banks (Shinkin) in Japan: Motives and Consequences. *Research Institute of Economy, Trade and Industry (RIETI) Discussion papers.* No. 06034.

International Finance Corporation. 2017. *MSME Finance Gap: Assessment of the Shortfalls and Opportunities in Financing Micro, Small and Medium Enterprises in Emerging Markets.* https://www.ifc.org/wps/wcm/connect/03522e90-a13d-4a02-87cd-9ee9a297b311/121264-WP-PUBLIC-MSMEReportFINAL.pdf?MOD=AJPERES&CVID=m5SwAQA.

Japan Small and Medium Enterprise (SME) Agency. 2019. *White Paper on Small and Medium Enterprises in Japan.* https://www.chusho.meti.go.jp/sme_english/whitepaper/whitepaper.html.

Kang, J. W. and A. Heshmati. 2008. Effect of credit guarantee policy on survival and performance of SMEs in Republic of Korea. *Small Business Economics.* 31(4). pp. 445–462.

Kim, S. S., H. Lee, T. W. Kessler, and M. S. Khan. 2021. Policies to Optimize the Performance of Credit Guarantee Schemes During Financial Crises. *ADB Briefs.* No. 167. https://www.adb.org/sites/default/files/publication/680196/adb-brief-167-credit-guarantee-schemes-financial-crises.pdf.

Korean Venture Capital Association. 2021. Summary Report (2020.4Q). http://www.kvca.or.kr/en/Program/summary_report/list.html?a_gb=eng&a_cd=4&a_item=0&sm=4_3.

KPMG. 2011. https://assets.kpmg/content/dam/kpmg/pdf/2013/06/KPMG-Credit-access-guarantees-public-asset-between-State-Market.pdf.

———. 2016. *Sri Lanka: Small and Medium-Sized Enterprises Line of Credit Project.* ADB Technical Assistance Consultants' Report.

Larraín, C. and J. Quiroz. 2006. *Estudio para el fondo de garantía de pequeños empresarios.* Banco del Estado. In Leone and Vento, eds. 2012. Washington, DC.

Levitsky, J. 1997. Credit Guarantee Schemes for SMEs—An International Review. *Small Enterprise Development.* 8(2). pp. 4–17.

Liang, L., B. Huang, C. Liao, and Y. Gao. 2017. The impact of SMEs' lending and credit guarantee on bank efficiency in South Korea. *Review of Development Finance.* 7(2). pp. 133–141. https://www.sciencedirect.com/science/article/pii/S1879933717300222.

Love, I., M. S. Martínez Pería, and S. Singh. 2013. Collateral Registries for Movable Assets: Does Their Introduction Spur Firms' Access to Bank Finance? *Policy Research Working Paper.* No. 6477. Washington, DC: World Bank.

Martín-García, R. and J. M. Santor. 2021. Public guarantees: a countercyclical instrument for SME growth. Evidence from the Spanish Region of Madrid. *Small Business Economics, Springer.* 56(1). pp. 427–449.

Michaelas, N., F. Chittenden, and P. Poutziouris. 1999. Financial policy and capital structure choice in UK SMEs: Empirical evidence from company panel data. *Small Business Economics.* 12(2). pp. 113–130.

Moody's Analytics. 2016. https://www.moodysanalytics.com/-/media/whitepaper/2016/seven-key-challenges-assessing%20small-medium-enterprises-sme-credit-risk.pdf.

Nadeem, T. and R. Rasool. 2018. Marketing: The Crucial Success Factor for Pakistan's Credit Guarantee Scheme. *ADBI Working Paper Series.* No. 909. Tokyo.

Neuberger, D. and S. Räthke-Döppner. 2008. Wirksamkeit von Landesbürgschaften und Bürgschaftsbanken: eine empirische Studie für Mecklenburg-Vorpommern. *Zeitschrift für öffentliche und gemeinwirtschaftliche Unternehmen.* 31(4). pp. 386–406.

Nguyen, B. and N. Canh. 2020. Formal and informal financing decisions of small businesses. *Small Business Economics.* 57. pp. 545–1567.

Organisation for Economic Co-operation and Development (OECD). 2000. Small and Medium-Sized Enterprises: Local Strength, Global Reach. *Policy Brief.* http://www.oecd.org/cfe/leed/1918307.pdf.

———. 2005. *Oslo Manual: Guidelines for Collecting and Interpreting Innovation Data.* Paris: OECD.

———. 2006. *The SME Financing Gap: Theory and Evidence. Financial Market Trends.* Paris.

———. 2009. *The Impact of the Global Crisis on SME and Entrepreneurship Financing and Policy Responses.* https://www.oecd.org/cfe/smes/theimpactoftheglobalcrisisonsmeandentrepreneurshipfinancing andpolicyresponses.htm.

———. 2010a. *Assessment of Government Support Programmes for SMEs' and Entrepreneurs' Access to Finance during the Crisis.* Paris: OECD.

———. 2010b. *Facilitating Access to Finance – Discussion Paper on Credit Guarantee Schemes.* https://www. oecd.org/global-relations/45324327.pdf.

———. 2011. Credit Guarantee Schemes: A tool to promote SME growth and innovation in the MENA region. *MENA-OECD Investment Programme Working Paper.*

———. 2013. *SME and Entrepreneurship Financing: The Role of Credit Guarantee Schemes and Mutual Guarantee Societies in Supporting Finance for Small and Medium-Sized Enterprises Final Report.* https://one.oecd.org/document/CFE/SME(2012)1/FINAL/en/pdf.

———. 2015. *New Approaches to SME and Entrepreneurship Financing: Broadening the Range of Instruments.* https://www.oecd.org/cfe/smes/New-Approaches-SME-full-report.pdf.

———. 2017. *Evaluating Publicly Supported Credit Guarantee Programmes for SMEs.* www.oecd.org/finance/ Evaluating-Publicly-Supported-Credit-Guarantee-Programmes-for-SMEs.pdf.

Oh, I., J. Lee, A. Heshmati, and G. Choi. 2009. Evaluation of credit guarantee policy using propensity score matching. *Small Business Economics.* 33(3). pp. 335–351.

Owens, J. V. and L. Wilhelm. 2017. *Alternative data transforming SME finance* (English). http://documents. worldbank.org/curated/en/701331497329509915/Alternative-data-transforming-SME-finance.

Pombo, P., H. Molina, and J. N. Ramírez Sobrino. 2015. *The Guarantee Systems: Keys for the Implementation.* Spanish Association of Accounting and Business Administration. Madrid.

Pompian, M. 2012. Regret Aversion Bias. In *Behavioral Finance and Wealth Management: How to Build Investment Strategies That Account for Investor Biases.* https://onlinelibrary.wiley.com/ doi/10.1002/9781119202400.ch22.

Riding, A. and G. Haines. 2001. Loan Guarantees: Costs of Default and Benefits to Small Firms. *Journal of Business Venturing.* 16(6). pp. 595–612.

Riding, A., J. Madill, and G. Haines. 2007. Incrementality of SME Loan Guarantees. *Small Business Economics.* 29(1–2). pp. 47–61.

Roper, S. 2009. *Credit Guarantee Schemes: a tool to promote SME growth and innovation in the MENA region.* 3rd MENA-OECD Working Group on SME Policy. United Kingdom: Warwick Business School. 26 October.

Saadani, Y., A. Zsofia, and R. Rocha. 2011. A Review of Credit Guarantee Schemes in the Middle East and North Africa Region. *World Bank Policy Research Working Paper*. 5612.

Schena, C. 2012. L'adeguatezza patrimoniale dei Confidi: profile normative e prospettive gestionali. In R. Locatelli, ed. Rischi, patrimonio e organizzazione nei Confidi, Associazione Ricerche su Imprese. Intermediari, Mercati – ARIME, Milan.

Schmidt, A. G. and M. van Elkan. 2010. *The Macroeconomic Benefits of German Guarantee Banks.* University of Trier.

Shinkin Central Bank. 2015. *Shinkin Central Bank Annual Report, 2014.* Tokyo.

Slotty. 2009. Financial constraints and the decision to lease – evidence from German SME. *Working Paper Series: Finance & Accounting.* No. 205. Goethe-Universität Frankfurt.

Small and Medium Enterprise Development Bank of Thailand. 2020. *SME Development Bank Annual Report 2020.* https://www.smebank.co.th/en/about/annual-report.

Stiglitz, J. E. and A. Weiss. 1981. Credit Rationing in Markets with Imperfect Information. *American Economic Review.* 71(3). pp. 393–410.

Thorburn, K. 2000. Bankruptcy auctions: costs, debt recovery, and firm survival. *Journal of Financial Economics.* 58(3). pp. 337–368.

Uesugi, I. and K. Sakai. 2005. The Special Credit Guarantee Program in Japan. https://www.rieti.go.jp/users/uesugi-iichiro/cf-workshop/pdf/uesugi-sakai.pdf#page=6.

Uesugi, I., K. Sakai, and G. M. Yamashiro. 2006. Effectiveness of Credit Guarantees in the Japanese Loan Market. *RIETI Discussion Paper Series.* No. 06-E-004. Tokyo.

———. 2010. The Effectiveness of Public Credit Guarantees in the Japanese Loan Market. *Journal of the Japanese and International Economies, Elsevier.* 24(4). pp. 457–480.

UK Department for International Development (DFID), Financial Sector Team, Policy Division. 2005. Do Credit Guarantees Lead to Improved Access to Financial Services? Recent Evidence from Chile, Egypt, India and Poland. London.

Valentin, A. and T. Henschel. 2013. Do guarantee banks affect SME lending? *International Journal of Entrepreneurship and Small Business.* 20(4). pp. 481–496.

Vienna Initiative. 2014. *Credit Guarantee Schemes for SME Lending in Central, Eastern and South-Eastern Europe.* Luxembourg: European Investment Bank.

Wilcox, J. and Y. Yasuda. 2008. Do Government Loan Guarantees Lower, or Raise, Banks' Non-Guaranteed Lending? Evidence from Japanese Banks. The World Bank Workshop Partial Credit Guarantees. Haas School of Business University of California, Berkeley, Faculty of Business Administration Tokyo Keizai University. 13–14 March.

World Bank. 2019a. *Knowledge Guide.* http://documents1.worldbank.org/curated/pt/193261570112901451/pdf/Secured-Transactions-Collateral-Registries-and-Movable-Asset-Based-Financing.pdf.

———. 2019b. *Ease of Doing Business.* https://www.doingbusiness.org/en/reports/global-reports/doing-business-2019.

World Federation of Exchanges. 2018. An Overview of WFE SME Markets. https://www.world-exchanges.org/storage/app/media/research/Studies_Reports/2018/WFE%20Overview%20of%20SME%20Markets%20Report%20October%202018.pdf.

Yildirim, D., O. Unal, and A. Gedikli. 2015. Financial Problems of Small and Medium-Sized Enterprises in Turkey. *International Journal of Academic Research in Business and Social Sciences.* 5(1). pp. 27–37.

Yoshino, N. and T. Hirano. 2011. Pro-Cyclicality of the Basel Capital Requirement Ratio and its Impact on Banks. *Asian Economic Papers.* 10(2). pp. 22–36.

Yoshino, N. and F. Taghizadeh-Hesary. 2014. An Analysis of Challenges Faced by Japan's Economy and Abenomics. *The Japanese Political Economy.* 40(3–4). pp. 37–62.

———. 2016a. Causes and Remedies of Japan's Long-lasting Recession: Lessons for China. *China & World Economy.* 24(2). pp. 23–47.

———. 2016b. Major challenges facing small and medium-sized enterprises in Asia and solutions for mitigating them. *ADBI Working Paper,* No. 564. Tokyo.

———. 2016c. Optimal Credit Guarantee Ratio for Asia. *ADBI Working Paper Series.* No. 586. Tokyo.

———. 2018a. The Role of SMEs in Asia and Their Difficulties in Accessing Finance. *ADBI Working Paper.* No. 911. Tokyo.

———. 2018b. Optimal Credit Guarantee Ratio for Small and Medium-Sized Enterprises' Financing: Evidence from Asia. *Economic Analysis and Policy.* https://doi.org/10.1016/j.eap.2018.09.011.

Zander, R., C. Miller, and N. Mhlanga. 2013. *Credit Guarantee Systems for Agriculture and Rural Enterprise Development.* Rome: Food and Agriculture Organization of the United Nations.

www.ingramcontent.com/pod-product-compliance
Lightning Source LLC
Chambersburg PA
CBHW050047220326
41599CB00045B/7312